CARING FOR CHILDREN AWAY FROM HOME

AP'

CARING FOR CHILDREN AWAY FROM HOME

Messages from Research

JOHN WILEY & SONS

Chichester • New York • Weinheim • Brisbane • Singapore • Toronto

Copyright © 1998 by   John Wiley & Sons Ltd,
Baffins Lane, Chichester,
West Sussex PO19 IUD, England

National 01243 779777
International (+44) 1243 779777
e-mail (for orders and customer service enquiries):
cs-books@wiley.co.uk
Visit our Home Page on http://www.wiley.co.uk
or http://www.wiley.com

Other Wiley Editorial Offices
John Wiley & Sons, Inc., 605 Third Avenue,
New York, NY 10158-0012, USA

WILEY-VCH Verlag GmbH, Pappelallee 3,
D-69469 Weinheim, Germany

Jacaranda Wiley Ltd, 33 Park Road, Milton,
Queensland 4064, Australia

John Wiley & Sons (Asia) Pte Ltd, 2 Clementi Loop #02-01,
Jin Xing Distripark, Singapore 129809

John Wiley & Sons (Canada) Ltd, 22 Worcester Road,
Rexdale, Ontario M9W lL1, Canada

ISBN 0-471-98475-2

Designed and typeset in Scala and Scala Sans by Kevin Mount
Printed and bound in Great Britain by BPC Ltd, Exeter
This book is printed on acid-free paper responsibly manufactured from sustainable forestry, in which at least two trees are planted for each one used for paper production.

Foreword

I am pleased to have the opportunity to commend this book to all interested in the care of those children and young people who are looked after by local authorities. I am sure it will prove to be a significant contribution to future thinking, practice and management for all who work in local authority social services and private and voluntary services and who provide care for children who live away from home.

The group of studies surveyed and summarised here was commissioned by the Department of Health to address key concerns arising from a series of public inquiries in the late 1980s and early 1990s, and to provide a balanced account of what residential care in the UK is like in the 1990s. This research came in the wake of the implementation of the *Children Act* 1989 and its Regulations and Guidance, which provided significant new safeguards for children living away from home. Additional government action to protect these children was taken with the publication of further guidance and the reports of the Support Force for Children's Residential Care. However, as Sir William Utting's report *People Like Us* highlights, residential care continues to have major problems today (Utting 1997).

The overview presents evidence that living away from home may be a significant component of the lives of some of our most vulnerable children. However, residential care can only provide good outcomes for these children if it is part of a co-ordinated, evidence-based and thoughtful service to children in need.

I urge all of you concerned about children and young people whose needs require special support from residential provision, health, education, careers and housing to use this book as a way of thinking about the effectiveness of your own services to children, and to consider how, by working with others, you might better meet the needs of the most vulnerable young people.

Children in need, especially those who live away from home, are the responsibility of all of us.

Paul Boateng Esq. MP
Parliamentary Under Secretary of State
Department of Health

This overview summarises a programme of research planned, commissioned and managed for the Department of Health by Dr Carolyn Davies with the strong support of John Rowlands. It has been prepared by Lesley Archer, Leslie Hicks, Michael Little and Kevin Mount with the help of an advisory group, the membership of which reflected the range of professionals involved with children whose care includes periods in residential settings. In addition, drafts were read by the researchers whose work contributed to the overview, by other academics and by policy makers and practitioners. Certain members of the advisory group also worked with other experts who were asked to help with the production of the *True for Us* exercises.

The advisory group

Carolyn Davies *Senior Principal Research Officer, Department of Health* (Chair)
Dorothy Alexander* *Children's Rights Officer, Durham Social Services*
Jane Allberry *Section Head for Looked After Children, Department of Health*
Ewan Anderson *Professor of Middle Eastern and Islamic Studies, University of Durham*
Celia Atherton* *Director, Research in Practice, Warren House, Dartington*
Susan Bailey *Consultant Adolescent Forensic Psychiatrist, Mental Health Services of Salford*
Valerie Brasse *Section Head for Looked After Children, Department of Health*
Roger Clough *Professor of Social Work, University of Lancaster*
Mike Craddock* *Service Manager, Children and Families Service, Devon Social Services*
Norman Duncan, *Branch Head Children's Services, Department of Health*
Elaine Farmer *Lecturer in Social Work, School for Policy Studies, University of Bristol*
Bill Hendley *Director of Social Services, Coventry*
Richard Hilditch* *Child Care Manager, North Lincolnshire Social Services*
Lynda Hoare *Social Services Inspector, Department of Health*
Steve Hart *Social Services Inspector, Department of Health*
Tine Hunt *Unit Manager, Chestnut Respite Unit, Lambeth Social Services*
Rob Hutchinson *Director of Social Services, Portsmouth*
Jean Packman *Centre for Social Policy, Warren House, Dartington*
Ann Phoenix *Department of Psychology, Birkbeck College, University of London*
David Quinton *Professor of Psycho-Social Development, University of Bristol*
John Rea Price *Director, National Children's Bureau*
John Rowlands *Social Services Inspector, Department of Health*
Richard Whipp *Deputy Director, Cardiff Business School, University of Wales*
Wendy Rose* *Senior Fellow, School of Social Work, University of Leicester*
Brian Sheldon *Director, Centre for Evidence-based Social Services, University of Exeter*
Also helped with True for Us *exercises*

Members joining for the development of the *True for Us* exercises were:
Ruth Hall   David Lane
Kathleen Lane   Dave Shipman
Mike Simm   Adrian Ward
Phil Youdon

Contents

Introduction

This publication is one of a series that summarises and disseminates the results of child care research funded by the Department of Health. Previous volumes have dealt with the experiences of children looked after (*Patterns and Outcomes in Child Placement*) and the effectiveness of the child protection process (*Child Protection:Messages from Research*). A future volume will bring together findings concerning the impact of the *Children Act* 1989 (the framing of which was much influenced by the first overview). The book in hand concentrates on the situation of children in care or accommodation living in residential settings.

During the past ten years the residential sector has been dogged by difficulty. Not all the ills have been of its own making: this publication argues that it should become more integrated into the range of health, education and social services organised on behalf of children in need; but so must the wider world bear some responsibility for the deficiencies that have been identified.

Government has responded in several ways. In 1991 it organised a seminar for the principal players in the field–policy makers, managers, practitioners, children and researchers included–in order to map a way forward. The decision to commission the programme of research reported here reflected the desire to establish a firm foundation of evidence on which to plan services away from the glare of unrepresentative scandal. The report, *Residential Care for Children*, also helped to pave the way forward by reviewing the post-war literature and identifying gaps in existing knowledge. Subsequently a Support Force for Children's Residential Care was created which, in an intentionally short life, produced several practical guides to help local authorities improve the management of residential care. There have also been the successive reports of Sir William Utting, and in the autumn of 1998 the response of a cross-department group of Ministers will be published which is likely to be tied into a series of wider developments emerging from the Government's Comprehensive Spending Review of its activities.

The new studies contribute in different ways, as the table over the page illustrates. Many have focused on the residential context. Whitaker and colleagues considered the culture and dynamics of children's homes continuing, with Brown and colleagues, a research tradition that can be traced to the beginning of the century. Sinclair and Gibbs conducted a comprehensive study to establish what might be the attributes of an effective residential setting. Berridge and Brodie returned to placements studied a decade earlier to see what had changed in the interim. Others followed specific groups of children, some of whom passed through residence (witness Farmer and Pollock's study of sexually abused and abusing children). Much information has come from following the progress of children after residence, for example as a result of the studies by Biehal, Clayden, Stein and Wade on leaving care and going missing. Management and training structures are also scrutinised in the studies by Whipp, Hill and their colleagues.

The studies extended to several types of placement. Most of the research looked into children's homes which form the bedrock of residence organised by the social services. A proportion were provided by the private sector. Sinclair and Gibbs mounted a separate investigation of this aspect of the work. There are also some secure units, again provided by local authorities or the Department of Health itself. These placements are sheltering children at the extreme end of the spectrum of need. There are also some therapeutic communities and other specialist treatment regimes included in the studies. Residence is a term encompassing many types of service.

The book has three principal components:
- an overview of the main messages of research
- a summary of each study included in the overview
- 'True for Us' exercises.

The overview essay is itself divided into three sections. The first sets the scene by describing the changing face of residence and some of its main challenges. The second links the messages from research from the 13 studies, looking at the children, the homes, the staff, management and training and connections between residence and the world outside. A general conclusion of the contributing studies seems to be acknowledgement of a need for a radical review of the sector. The essay ends, therefore, by setting out a framework to encourage reflection of a kind that may produce the necessary development.

The overview essay has other components. There are recommendations for good practice written by the researchers themselves. There are also pointers to methods that will enable local authorities and other provider agencies to understand the nature of their business–whom they are trying to help; what they offer on behalf of children; how effective are those services.

Every programme of research has shortcomings. The current level of understanding of children in need has not permitted very precise trials to establish which programmes work for which children. By concentrating on residence–which had become a neglected area of research–these studies could not be used as a basis for comparisons with other types of provision–which are no doubt beset with similar difficulties. There is not much in the book about residential

Studies in the programme

Title	Authors	Numbers of homes and of children included in the studies
Moving On: Young people and leaving care schemes, 1995	Nina Biehal Jasmine Clayden Mike Stein Jim Wade, University of York	They studied 30 young people leaving residential care.
Secure Treatment Outcomes, 1998	Roger Bullock Michael Little Spencer Millham, Dartington Social Research Unit	They studied 204 young people who passed through 2 long-stay secure treatment units.
Sexually Abused and Abusing Children in Substitute Care, 1998	Elaine Farmer Sue Pollock, University of Bristol	They screened 250 young people to identify 21 sexually abused or abusing individuals in 18 homes.
Going Missing: Young people absent from care (The York study of Going Missing), 1998	Jim Wade Nina Biehal Jasmine Clayden Mike Stein, University of York	They collected information on 127 children who went missing from 32 children's homes.
Children's Homes Revisited, 1998	David Berridge Isabelle Brodie, University of Luton	They studied 12 homes looking after 77 children.
Making Residential Care Work: Structure and culture in children's homes, 1998	Elizabeth Brown Roger Bullock Caroline Hobson Michael Little, Dartington Social Research Unit	They studied 9 homes caring for 65 children.
Private Children's Homes, 1998	Ian Gibbs Ian Sinclair, University of York	They studied 12 homes caring for 49 children.
A Life Without Problems? The achievements of a therapeutic community, 1995	Michael Little Siobhan Kelly, Dartington Social Research Unit	They studied 60 children passing through a therapeutic community.
Children's Homes: A study in diversity (The York effectiveness study), 1998	Ian Sinclair Ian Gibbs, University of York	They studied 48 homes looking after 223 residents.
Working in Children's Homes: Challenges and complexities (The York study of cultures), 1998	Dorothy Whitaker Lesley Archer Leslie Hicks, University of York	They studied 34 homes looking after 245 children.
Evaluating Residential Care Training, 1998	Dione Hills Camilla Child Julie Hills Vicky Blackburn, Tavistock Institute	They studied 89 residential staff on 8 Dip. SW programmes.
The External Management of Children's Homes by Local Authorities, 1999	Richard Whipp Ian Kirkpatrick Martin Kitchener Dianne Owen, University of Cardiff Business School	They studied the management of homes in 12 local authorities.

life beyond the personal social services for children although there is much to be learned from neighbouring sectors.

The book continues the tradition of using the studies from a distinct programme of research. As such it puts to one side a considerable and highly authoritative literature on residential care. It may be helpful to readers to look also at a previous Department of Health review of the literature, *Residential Care for Children: A Review of the Research*, published in 1993.

The reader will note that the overview essay uses the word children, except in those cases when an observation is solely concerned with young people. This choice has been made largely for the sake of brevity but it reflects the obligations society has to all children up to the age of 18. Given the variety of placements covered by the research, finding the right word to describe the entire sector has proved problematic. The difficulty is compounded by a growing doubt that 'children's home' is a useful descriptor in an age when services are being required to be much more tightly matched to the needs of children.

The general aim has been to provide an accessible document that will encourage widespread reflection on how services with a residential component can support children in need. The aim is to inform everyone working with vulnerable children and ultimately to enhance the welfare of children.

Clearing the ground

Residential care was once at the fulcrum of services for children in need. Today it falls short of society's expectations. There is manifestly smaller demand for it and too great a proportion of the few who experience it seem to suffer as a result; they certainly do not benefit as much as they should.

Argument about the usefulness of residential care has been fairly constant in the post war period and there have been big changes as a consequence. There is much less residence than there used to be; placements are smaller and there are cheaper (if not necessarily better value) alternatives. There has not been much scope for careful planning though. More often those responsible for providing residential care have been driven to respond to changing conditions, sometimes in the aftermath of scandal or in the train of new social policy, but more generally in the context of a loss of belief in the value of communal living. Today, while there continues to be disagreement about the benefits of children's homes, secure units, hostels and other residential placements, most commentators would say that the time has come for radical, well-planned development.

If the change is to be for the better, it is important not to perpetuate an out-of-date view of residence. There is nothing left in the argument that the sector has unique characteristics. Residential settings are no longer distinctive by their size; they cannot claim to be sole possessors of an answer to the problems of children in need, collectively or individually. Nor can residential care hope to do good in isolation; it has come to depend for its well being on the wider service system. This much is clear from the evidence presented in these pages.

One of the elements of a radical review might be at the level of general confidence. Residence has undoubtedly done many children good. It would represent a significant step forward if everyone involved in providing services for children was convinced about the nature of the residential sector's contribution to the overall task. Given the scale of the problems of some troubled children and the wise uncertainty about what can be done to help them, few suggest that it has nothing to offer at all; the key questions concern what benefits, for whom and under what circumstances. Again, much of the research described here tries to identify the conditions in which residence can be shown to be beneficial. That investigation will continue but for our knowledge to improve, new living environments will need to be developed, experimented with and tested. Change may be radical; a radical expectation would be that not all of it will work.

So, an important theme in all that follows is that the residential care sector has undeniably hard realities to face; like the children it tries to help, it poses society a number of problems, some very thorny indeed. This book is not, therefore, a comforting read. It describes much that is wrong with residence, mitigated to a degree by some strong indications of how it can be improved. It also suggests a framework within which a change of approach, acceptable to critics and supporters of the sector, might be achieved.

The intention has been to set out the research evidence in a way that will encourage the reader to turn to the studies themselves. Summarisers are only too aware of the potential shortcomings of boxes and bullet points; please do not imagine they can tell the whole story.

First, it is necessary to say something more about how residence has changed over the years, about the current services' context and what can sensibly be expected of residential interventions in the new millennium.

Children in need

All children have needs; for love, shelter, security and more. Most children's needs are met by family and friends. Some needs–for example for good health and education–are addressed by universal services provided by the state, often through a single type of agency. A smaller proportion of children have more complex needs that handicap their ability to lead an ordinary life. Their needs are usually the consequence of several problems, for instance the interaction over time between where they live, their family relations, their health or education. These children's needs demand specialist services, sometimes called Part III services after the relevant section of the *Children Act* 1989. A single agency is seldom able to address the needs of these children.

Local and health authorities have a duty to identify children in need. Methods of identifying such children remain somewhat crude, and scientific approaches to the question are still in development. The previous overview *Child Protection: Messages from Research* put the figure nationally at 600,000. Some commentators have said it is lower, some higher. The figure is not fixed. It is something on which society must decide, ideally using consistently rigorous methods.

Children in need of residential care

A small proportion of children in need can benefit from services which include residential care. Another perspective is to ask 'who needs residential care?'. If the potential catchment is widened beyond children in need, other groups of children who might benefit from residence can be identified. For example, a proportion of the children whose parents work abroad but who otherwise lead fairly unremarkable lives appear to benefit from residential settings. Such children are beyond the scope of this publication, although the findings may have relevance for some of the residential settings in which they live, such as boarding schools.

What to call a placement

Most of the placements studied by the research were called children's homes, a very general term, which, as will be seen, includes a range of services. The evidence presented here may lead the reader to think that the description is out of date. It is retained here because it was used so extensively in the period leading up to this research, but that is not to imply any endorsement of its relevance: where the evidence relates to all residential placements in personal social services for children, including secure accommodation and therapeutic communities, the all encompassing term 'residence' is preferred.

How residential care has been changing

Residential care has long been a significant aspect of the public provision for children. There have been hospitals for the sick; asylums–once a tender term–for the mentally ill; boarding schools to educate; Poor Law institutions to shelter the destitute; approved schools and borstals to reform the delinquent. But, as the second column of figures in the table over the page illustrates, for every 100 children living in residential settings today, just six will be in places primarily designed for children in need looked after by Social Services Departments.

The numbers in the table indicate the place of children's homes in the context of the overall residential provision. They also reveal how rapid the decline has been. When the new century begins, there will be just half the number of children in residence there were 30 years ago. With the exception of special schools, the startling slump in numbers has affected all sectors–education and health as well as social care–and it extends to many parts of the globe, certainly

Residential care for children in need

How is residential care to be defined in the context of modern children's services? In essence, it is a place where children live and sleep, for at least one night. As a rule, the adults who look after the children will be employed for that purpose but they will have their own homes to go to when their shift comes to an end (in rare instances that 'home' may be on the same campus as the children's home). Children in need live in a variety of settings, but *only* children in need live in the sort of residential care described in this overview and there are nearly always at least two children resident at any one time.

The nearest relation to residential care is foster care. There has been some blurring of the boundaries between the two of late but there remain important differences. Foster parents use their own home to shelter the children. They may be employed to look after the child but they will live in the house and will continue to do so after the child has moved on. Foster parents' own children live in a third of foster placements. In terms of children's experiences, the majority of foster homes are effectively small children's homes run by foster parents in their own household.

Some factors that once defined residential care are no longer useful. Size would have been a distinguishing feature but an average children's home now has just seven residents and about half the placements are smaller than the larger foster homes. Payment for the complexity of the task (as opposed to the cost of looking after the child) would once have applied only to residence, but no longer. Nor is length of stay a distinguishing feature. There is little to choose between the mean length of stay of children in foster and residential homes.

not just England and Wales. On the other hand, within the European Union, most member states, including Germany, Italy and the Netherlands have more residential care for looked after children than they do foster care.

Within children's services the change has been particularly marked. In the early 1980s David Berridge studied 20 children's homes selected to be representative of the country as a whole. When he and his colleague, Isabelle Brodie, returned to the same places ten years later, 16 had closed and two others were on the brink. Only four of the 136 residential care staff were doing similar work with the same employer. It is very difficult to think of another social context where similar results could be found.

A decline in numbers is often taken to indicate a decline in quality. Because research into the outcomes of public sector services is so recent, the truth of this assumption in relation to residential care will never be known. But there have been obvious problems. A succession of public inquiries has highlighted staffing problems, a failure to protect children from maltreatment and a general sense of unhappiness. Then research studies of the sort at the core of this overview have uncovered disquieting evidence about bullying, sexual harassment, offending, running away and inadequate supervision of sexually abusing young people. A superficial reading might destroy what little confidence remains in the value of residence.

Children's homes in the context of residence for children

About 130,000 children will sleep in a residential setting tonight. Two-thirds of them will be in ordinary boarding schools and another 20,000 in Special Education contexts. Each night there are 12,000 children in hospitals, two-fifths more than will be in children's homes.

Number in thousands (aged 0-18 in England and Wales)

Context	1971	1996
Children's homes	41	7
Boarding special schools	21	21
Provision for children with disabilities	14	2
Young offender institutions	2	2
Boarding schools (not special)	141	84
Hospitals	16	12
Total	235	128

The common denominator between these different contexts is the decline in numbers. Overall, the fall has been 45% since the 1971 survey by Peter Moss. For children's homes the proportion is 82%; in other words for every six children in residence in 1971 there is just one today.

Certainly only the most complacent observer would deny that there are serious problems in the residential sector or that some places are functioning much better than others. The question is what can be done to improve matters generally without undermining the efforts of those establishments already doing well.

Whatever its deficiencies, local authorities have not been able to do without residential care. Cliffe and Berridge found that the decision to close the residential provision in Warwickshire resulted in specialist places for the most difficult children having to be purchased at some distance from their family, school and neighbourhood–not always a good outcome.

On the other hand, although many local authorities have continued to provide residential services, few have reaped consistent rewards from their investment. The research teams contributing to this overview measured effectiveness in different ways. Some, like Sinclair and Gibbs and Berridge and Brodie made a statistical division and found ordinary children's homes to be extraordinarily varied in quality. Some, like Brown and colleagues, measured outcomes of homes

Scandal

Scandals in residential care are not new. In the nineteenth century, public schools faced continual disorder from unruly pupils and, in child welfare settings, physical assault, neglect and occasional sexual abuse seem to have been almost an expectation of residential life. The establishment of Children's Departments in 1948 raised standards in children's homes but the violent undercurrent survived in some larger establishments, such as approved schools, until the 1970s when tolerance decreased and suspicions of abuse were confirmed by independent scrutiny. Several sexual abuse scandals not only became public, but were also followed by judicial inquiries, closures and criminal prosecutions. The inquiries showed:

1. Abuse can occur in all types of residential settings–in large reception and assessment units (such as the Kincora Boys' Home in Northern Ireland), in children's homes (such as in Leicestershire, Staffordshire and Clwyd), in specialised treatment centres (such as Bryn Alyn) and in independent boarding schools (such as Crookham Court).

2. Abuse is often accompanied by a regime in which perpetrators control those likely to speak out by threats or encouraging other deviant behaviour which makes them fearful of external scrutiny.

3. Repressive regimes make disclosure by victims and innocent bystanders difficult; outsiders are often more successful at starting the process that exposes the truth.

4. Sexual abuse is not just perpetrated by isolated individuals; in some cases abusing staff have known one another and moved between homes.

Recommendations to increase children's safety have been made in the 1997 Utting Report, *People Like Us*. Terrible as these abuses have been, the majority of children have not been affected. Most misery in residence is a consequence of other children's behaviour as the following pages relate.

against pre-defined criteria and discovered that a third were 'good', the same proportion as were 'poor'. Others monitored the progress of children experiencing residence. Farmer and Pollock found that four out of 21 did well; Little and Kelly that 14 out of 60 achieved good outcomes, and Bullock and colleagues that nearly half (46%) of 204 were reasonably successful. Of course, the same results show that whatever the criteria, most do not fare very well.

Varied outcomes nevertheless tell us that it is possible for the job to be done well. As Sir William Utting points out in *People Like Us*, 'There are many excellent institutions–and people–caring for children who live away from home'. For Utting, the way forward is to create environments of overall excellence. The evidence here suggests that it is possible to learn from the good in order to improve the less than good. However local authorities set about the job of creating environments of overall excellence, they will want to explore two general issues:

- the place of residence in the wider scheme of services for children in need

- the expectations society may reasonably have for children in need who are placed in residential care.

The work of children's homes

The work of children's homes has become very diverse. Department of Health statistics show that just over a third (34%) are solely concerned with looking after children away from home. But most have other functions:

Respite	35%
Services for children with disability	28%
Specialism with difficult adolescents	22% (including 2% with secure accommodation)
Observation and assessment	19%
Hostel provision	13%
Education services	12%

There is overlap between different types of services. For example, some respite provision is devoted to disabled children and some observation centres also provide education. So the figures do not add up to 100.

The place of residence in the wider scheme of services

Even when it is experienced for only a few months, residential care can become a defining characteristic of a child in need. From the perspective of those working in children's homes, residence may seem to be the primary influence on a child's long-term well-being. Yet relatively few children in need leave the family home, never mind spend time in residential care. Furthermore, all residential placements are now combined with several other interventions, from health, education and social services, each of which has the potential to contribute to positive outcomes. Another important contextual consideration is the place residential care can usefully play in a child's development at different moments between birth and early adulthood. Now to take each of these perspectives in turn.

WHICH CHILDREN IN NEED SPEND TIME IN RESIDENCE?

When the progress of a cohort of children in need known to social services is tracked, it is found that no more than one in sixty finds his or her way into the children's homes, therapeutic communities and secure units that were the subject of research reviewed for this publication. Indeed, fewer than one in twenty of such children in need is ever looked after away from home. Most continue to live with relatives while they are helped by health, education or social services–and a substantial number, probably in the region of a quarter of a million, seem to manage without any intervention at all (as yet, little is known about their circumstances).

It is well known that about half the 30,000 children who are newly looked after by the state each year are away from home for no longer than six weeks, (although about 4,000 of the 15,000 experiencing such a swift reunion are destined to have a second period of care or accommodation). Nearly all of these short-stay cases go to foster placements; about 3,200 will live in residential settings only and another 150 will experience both.

It is well documented, too, that residential care is increasingly regarded as being the preserve of children looked after for longer periods. While this is largely the case, 9,500 children looked after for six weeks or more will live only in foster homes. Another 750 will move between different types of placement, leaving some 3,500 who will experience only residential placements. These are the children who will have most concerned the researchers contributing to this overview. The diagram over the page illustrates the pattern.

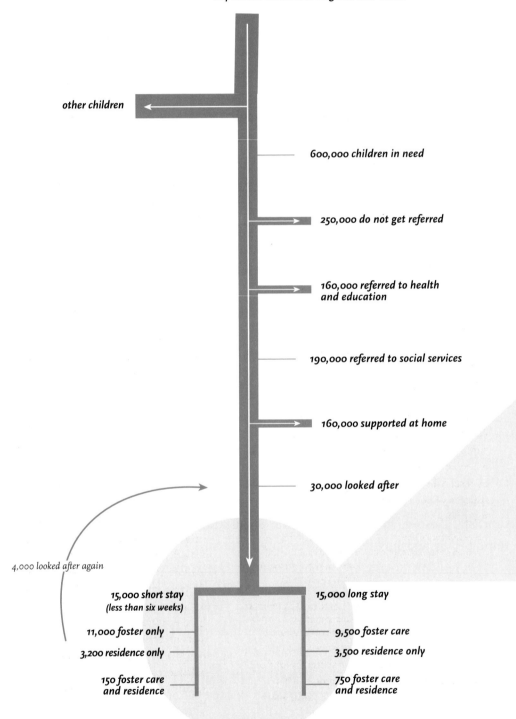

11.4 million children in England and Wales

other children

600,000 children in need

250,000 do not get referred

160,000 referred to health
and education

190,000 referred to social services

160,000 supported at home

30,000 looked after

4,000 looked after again

15,000 short stay
(less than six weeks)

11,000 foster only

3,200 residence only

150 foster care
and residence

15,000 long stay

9,500 foster care

3,500 residence only

750 foster care
and residence

The most reliable picture of children in need rests on what is known from following the progress of groups of children consecutively–the so-called 'movie' picture. Since there are no complete cohorts on which to rely, this picture has been assembled from several sources. Wherever possible, assumptions based on one set of data have been tested against another. That said, there is a scarcity of information on the early stages of children's services provision and research soon to be completed may challenge the current interpretation of the top part of the diagram. Sources used here include audit data from local authorities who have made a rapid evaluation of their work (Dartington has accumulated information on 5,000 children in need this way); central government statistics (for example the Department of Health's annual report on children looked after) and longitudinal research cohorts (eg, Dartington's recent studies *Children Going Home* and *From Care to Accommodation*).

Ethnicity

Evidence on the the ethnic origins of children in need remains sketchy. There is much uncertainty about the principal patterns but it is likely that about one in ten children looked after are from a minority ethnic group. If this figure is accurate, it would mean that there are fewer children from an ethnic minority in care or accommodation than ten years ago when Bebbington and Miles concluded that single race children from ethnic minorities were not over represented among children entering care, but that mixed race children were (by more than two and half times).

Jane Rowe and colleagues, also looking at the situation before the *Children Act*, found that a child from an ethnic minority was no more likely to be placed in residence than in a foster home (although there was considerable variation between authorities). Today, the available evidence suggests that children from minority ethnic groups are slightly less likely to be fostered and slightly more likely to experience movement between residential and foster settings.

There is not a great variation in the proportions of children from minority ethnic groups in residence found in the studies covered in this overview. Differences are as likely to reflect the local authorities included in each investigation, the quality of recording by professionals and the methods used by researchers (evidence collected directly from children will be different from anything gleaned from files). Thus:

Sinclair and Gibbs	8% of the 223 children
Bullock and Colleagues	22% of the 204 children (18% of the 121 in care or accommodation)
Berridge and Brodie	12% of the 77 children
Farmer and Pollock	13% of the 96 children who had been abused and/or were sexually abusive.

Putting children from different minority ethnic groups in a single category is unhelpful, not least because it hides important differences. This variation was found by Bullock and colleagues:

African-Caribbean	10%
African-Caribbean English	3%
African-Caribbean Asian	1%
African English	1%
Asian (Sikh)	1%
Asian (other)	2%
Asian-English	2%
Turkish	1%

Foster placements

As the discussion about definitions of homes makes clear, the distinction between residence and foster care is becoming blurred. About one foster child in six is the only child in the placement. About one in three will be the only foster child but the foster parents' own children will be living there too. That means roughly half live with other foster children *and* the offspring of the foster parents, making at least three children in the household altogether. Given the volume of cases being dealt with by foster care, it seems probable that more children live in large foster homes than in small children's homes.

Gender, length of stay, placement type

Most of the studies reported a slightly higher proportion of boys in residential care. Generally speaking, girls have a much higher chance of being fostered (three in four of all admissions compared to one in three of the boys) and a reduced chance of going into residence (one in five of all admissions compared to one in three for the boys). This uneven distribution does not seem to be explained by length of stay since boys remain looked after for no longer than girls.

Sexual abuse, gender, placement

Since the 1980s, professional awareness about sexual abuse has greatly increased. Farmer and Pollock estimate that some form of sexual maltreatment or abusing behaviour is an issue in the lives of about 12,000 of the 30,000 children newly looked after each year. Some of these children were sexually abused, some were sexual abusers, some were both. Girls accounted for nearly two-thirds of the victims but only a quarter of those instigating the maltreatment. The sensitivity of the subject matter tends to mean that sample sizes are too small to make broad generalisations, but it is possible that abusing children have a greater chance of being placed in foster care and abused children in residence.

RESIDENCE IN THE CONTEXT OF OTHER SERVICES FOR CHILDREN IN NEED

The *Children Act* 1989 introduced the concept of a continuum of services. The continuum model encourages local and health authorities to treat services as complementary rather than compartmentalised or even in opposition. By this means, social services departments have been encouraged to consider how residential care and foster placements together can achieve desirable ends for children looked after, rather than being driven to ask which one is better. Similarly, rather than making an issue of the relative merits of family support services and out of home care, the continuum model makes it easier for the advantages of both to be harnessed, particularly since it allows residence to be used as a means of family support.

A continuum of services

The impulse of philanthropists like Barnardo and Stephenson was to rescue children in need by building institutions*. With the passage of time, alternatives to residence, such as foster care and emigration, were sought. Later still, great efforts began to be made to make it unnecessary for children to leave home at all. This development process has its legacy in the way today's professionals think about responding to children's needs.

The concept of a continuum of services represents a different perspective on the same subject. The diagram below illustrates the idea. At one end of the continuum are services for children supported away from home; at the other those for children who live with parents. There are several options in between, including respite for the child from relatives or for relatives from the child. Children can move from one point on the continuum to another as their needs change. Services are only included when there is evidence that in combination with other interventions they can make a contribution to alleviating children's needs.

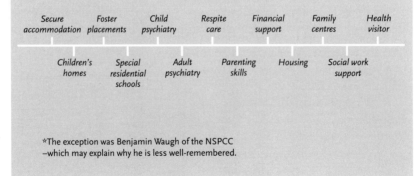

| Secure accommodation | Foster placements | Child psychiatry | Respite care | Financial support | Family centres | Health visitor |
| | Children's homes | Special residential schools | Adult psychiatry | Parenting skills | Housing | Social work support |

*The exception was Benjamin Waugh of the NSPCC
—which may explain why he is less well-remembered.

RESIDENTIAL CARE IN THE CONTEXT OF OTHER LIFE EXPERIENCES

Just as it can be said that a small proportion of children looked after stay long in residential settings, so those who remain in residential settings for a long time will nevertheless only spend a small part of their lives there. Most children going into residential care do not arrive until adolescence and eventually move on, usually to live with relatives. Others will go to foster homes or to various forms of independent living. Children who stay the longest in residential care ordinarily do not stay for more than six or seven of their 21 childhood years; for them residence is potentially a vital but never an all-encompassing contribution.

One child's experience of residence

The Little and Kelly study was partly written by one of the residents of the Caldecott therapeutic community in Kent. As the diagram illustrates, it was Siobhan Kelly's fourth residential placement, so she had spent more of her early years in a residential setting than most. Yet, important as it may have been, residential care has taken up a small proportion of her life: for fewer than a quarter of her nights up to the age of 20 she slept in a residential bed and much of what contributed to a successful care career outcome–her behaviour improved and she eventually gained a place at university–was attributable to other agencies, such as education and health, and to other placements, including foster care.

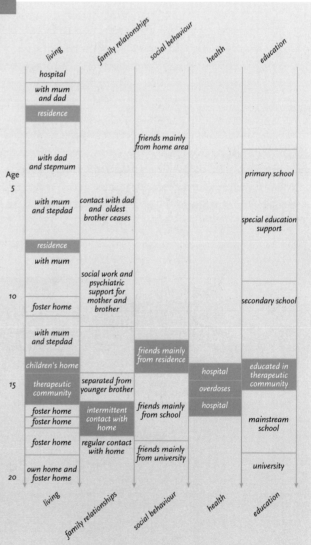

It may be helpful to consider the research findings and the recommendations for policy and practice development that flow from the evidence just described. As local and health authorities seek to create environments of overall excellence, it may be of use to know exactly which children in need residence is seeking to help, **A** (page 12), what other services will be necessary if stated objectives are to be achieved, **B** (page 14) and how the package of services will dovetail with a child's previous development and future aspirations, **C** (page 15). The next diagram hints at how the three perspectives converge on practice.

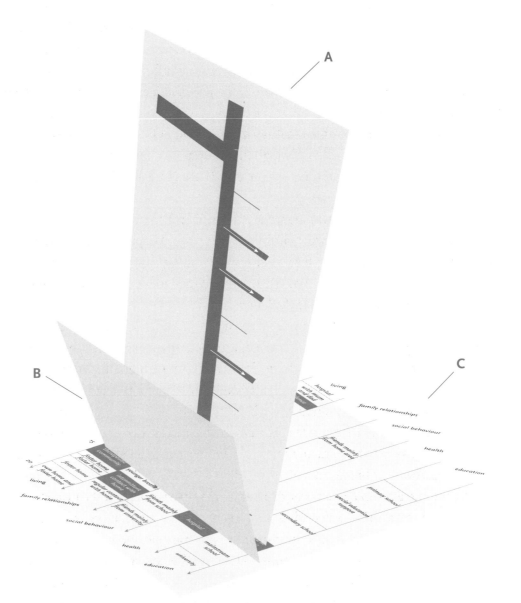

Reasonable expectations for children placed in residence

More so than in the past, residence has to be seen in the context of complicated arrangements involving the continuum of services just described and of efforts by the state to share the care of children with parents. Research suggests that many of these changes have been for the better but that it remains extremely difficult to help children who have to be supported away from home for long periods. These are the older, more damaged children; change on their behalf almost certainly demands a systematic review of what realistically can be achieved.

To illustrate the point: if it is an objective of local authority care and accommodation to enable children to enjoy better relations with their relatives (and for a significant proportion to return to live with relatives), should children's homes aspire to ordinary patterns of child development or to patterns which may be more typical for children in need? Given that a significant proportion of children looked after arrive with multiple and severe deficits, how long will it take to bring their development within normal range? If half the children entering residential placements stay for less than six weeks, should expectations for them be different from those held for that small proportion– about five in every hundred looked after–for whom the state effectively, if not legally, becomes the parent?

For the typical child looked after, the extremes of their experience are easy to judge. It is, for example, unacceptable that children in the public care should be victims of abuse–emotional, physical or sexual–inflicted by carers or other children with whom they live. Nor can it be right that children should become delinquent as a result of being looked after.

For the very difficult child, on the other hand, ordinary outcomes are less clear. Is it progress for a child convicted of a grave crime, such as murder, arson or rape, to commit a minor offence, such as shoplifting, on release from residential care? If a child who frequently runs away from home subsequently stays away from a children's home in which he or she is resident, has the situation improved or deteriorated? If a sexually abusing child has an orthodox sexual relationship with someone of his or her own age, should children's homes impose sanctions or breathe a sigh of relief?

Before one attempts to answer these everyday questions from the evidence the research teams have collected, it may help to be reminded of the constraints within which children's homes must operate. For example, there are legal and moral limitations: residential care must act within the law, abiding not only by the *Children Act* 1989 but also education and health and safety legislation, as well as any associated guidelines. Second, there is a moral expectation on the part of the country, the local and health authority and neighbourhood in which the placement is situated. Public expectations on behalf of residence and the children looked after can be unrealistic; for example, the hope that children's homes can become an invisible part of the infrastructure of a local community or that the residents will always be quiet, well-spoken and well behaved. Such decorum is difficult enough for typical adolescents to achieve, let alone those in need.

Increasingly, personal social services, like most public sector agencies, will listen to consumers' expectations. These may contradict one another. Parents' wishes will not always coincide with those of their children; adolescents may want to get away from home when their parents wish them to stay or decide to return when their parents were beginning to enjoy their independence. But research has shown that, regardless of background or circumstances, parental aspirations for their children are remarkably consistent. Nearly all parents want their children to be fit and healthy and to do well at school. If anything, they have higher hopes than local authorities who have greater resources to call upon for the children they look after. It would not be inconsistent to require professionals to raise their aspirations for the children for whom they have responsibility and to be more realistic about the outcomes that can be achieved within specified time periods.

The judgement of practitioners also bears upon the objectives for residence. In setting targets for children's residential care, it is necessary to reflect on available skills and resources. The size of the sector, the buildings available, replacement costs, the skills of the workforce, the likely support for young people on leaving all bear on the potential benefits.

A final influence is the available evidence. What ordinarily happens to different groups of children in need, with or without experience of the interventions administered by personal social services, remains largely unknown, but the experiences of children looked after are now well recorded. This publication adds a little more to our knowledge.

Each of these dimensions is subject to change. New laws are passed; guidance is revised; there are marked shifts in the moral climate and priorities are added to or subtracted from the skill base. As more is learned, so new questions are raised about past practice and our expectations for children in need shift accordingly. In such a climate nothing should be taken for granted.

Considering the evidence

The opening pages make the case for a major review of the place of residence in the continuum of services available to children in need. The closing pages describe a framework that should help local and health authorities to set about such a review. In between is a summary of the evidence from the programme of research, giving emphasis wherever possible to relevant messages and themes.

The evidence is divided into five sections, in turn dealing with:

- The children
- The homes
- Staff and their tasks
- Management, inspection and training
- Residence in its wider context

Information under each heading is separated into two main strands. Main themes are explored in the body of the essay. The column to the right of the main text is used for recommendations the research teams have made for the development of residential care. Cumulatively they should provide an avenue that may encourage a local authority to promote a rather different attitude to the residential sector and to enhance the quality of practice within it.

The children

Children in residence are a small, unusual sub-group of all children in need and a different, small sub-group of all children. On the whole, children who spend periods in residence have more complex and demanding problems than those who remain at home with relatives. Bullock and colleagues found that nearly all the most difficult and disturbed young people in England and Wales are placed in secure residential settings. Bristol found that just under a third of sexually abused and abusing children looked after went to a residential home. Little and Kelly found that continued demand for specialist therapeutic settings reflected a feeling among professionals that family contexts were unsuitable for some damaged children, or that the children themselves would not choose to live in a foster home.

While generalisations of this kind are rather unreliable, it can be said with some confidence that the children in residential homes present many challenges. Residential care is not the cause of their problems– although a badly run home will aggravate rather than ameliorate them: their problems are the burden society presents to residence.

Information is collected on each child in need in large quantities. Much of it is intended to help clarify threshold decisions about whether a child is in need or whether significant harm has been done. Information is also needed for placement decisions: who should be looked after and who should remain at home; how long should children stay and who can benefit from residence. Unfortunately, relatively little of what is collected is likely to travel with the child. A practitioner may assemble a social history to determine what kind of residential care is wanted, but then fail to pass on vital information when a placement is found. Among a group of 36 about whom there were serious concerns regarding sexual abuse, the Bristol team found that in 15 cases information was not passed on and that in another six significant detail had been omitted. Similar shortcomings were evident among groups of sexual abusers. There remains a tendency to rely on conversation and for residential social workers to avoid reading files lest they prejudge the child.

This column makes 24 suggestions ★ for tackling some of the weaker points of residence. All are drawn from the research studies and should be of interest to those working inside and outside the sector

★ I
Tools for collecting information about children in need, particularly those long in care or accommodation, have improved in recent years. For example, the Department of Health's *Looking After Children* materials provide a means of assembling essential background information, as well as data about personal development known to be conducive to good outcomes. The forms travel with the child, relieving practitioners at successive placements of the need to open a new record and risk shedding important information along the way.

Better outcomes will be achieved if information about children looked after and their families is properly communicated to all those involved. Residential social workers and other carers may benefit from being trained in the collection, interpretation and presentation of this information, in terms of what it means for the supervision and day to day care of the child and work with the family.

Categories of children in residence

There is no definitive classification of the children who find themselves in residential homes. Each study presents a different formulation, but Whitaker and colleagues put it most plainly in a list of characteristics staff are likely to encounter:

- chaotic behaviour and poor impulse control, including proneness to harm others or destroy property
- fearfulness of going to school or of the prospect of leaving care
- a sense of being lost, of having no-one and having no future
- persistent and continuing offending
- inappropriate sexual behaviour, ranging from sexualised behaviour to prostitution
- difficult relations with parents, ranging from concern about health, for example when a lone mother is hospitalised, to outright rejection.

It should be the case that the further down the map on p.8 that one looks, the more will be found the characteristics reported by Whitaker and colleagues and each should be more serious.

Information could include as much about children's personal strengths as it does about their weaknesses, when there is ample evidence in the studies to suggest that the former can be used as a means of overcoming the latter. Against a list of residents' behavioural and emotional problems, Whitaker and colleagues set out their personal strengths, such as competence, courage, sensitivity to others and a capacity for humour. Using the *Looking After Children* materials, Sinclair and Gibbs found that residents scored high in their growth and development, the majority were said by professionals to take reasonably good care of their appearance and to be reasonably well behaved, and the ability of three-quarters of them to care for themselves was described as good.

However the information is assembled, the range of difficulties posed by children in residential care has tended to resist clinical classification. Nearly all have emotional disorders and there is a high incidence of conduct disorder too, but the manifestation of these problems demands more than psychiatric assessment. Some of those received by children's homes will have been convicted of an offence but the fearfulness, sense of abandonment and alienation and the chaotic nature of the behaviour identified by the York study of cultures demand more than a youth justice intervention can provide. The Bristol team report that among two-fifths (38%) of children newly looked after there is a concern about sexual abuse or abusing behaviour but, combined with problems under the general headings of self-harm, delinquency and education, that it warrants much more than the involvement of a social worker. Children looked after in residence have a tendency to go missing; two fifths (43%) in the study by Wade and colleagues. Certain broad patterns are nevertheless apparent, as the following summary in the York effectiveness study illustrates:

★ 2

Two studies showed how information about risks and protective factors can be used to make a prognosis of a child's future life chances. Such a prognosis can be a valuable tool in fashioning an effective intervention.

Information passed from professional to professional can be used to predict outcomes in all areas of the child's life. This exercise is likely to encourage a realistic expectation about the future and help to tailor the intervention to the specific needs of the child.

The benefits of careful recording

The *Looking After Children* materials are now widely used by local authority social services departments and have been found particularly useful in residential contexts which support children for lengthy periods. The tools are primarily designed for one-to-one work with children but Sinclair and Gibbs aggregated the data with the following results:

The proportion of children scoring	High *and*	Low *in each area*
Health (growth and development)	96	4
Identity (self-esteem)	23	77
Presentation (communication skills)	58	42
Emotional development (problems)	70	30
Self Care (ability to care for oneself)	76	24
Education and work (attainment)	34	66
Family and friends (emotional ties)	63	37

Residential centres can use *Looking After Children* to judge their population against this national benchmark. It would be realistic to look for small improvements in one or more of the areas described, depending upon the priorities of the local and health authorities and of the residential centre itself. Patterns will vary according to the particular use of residential care and, consequently, of the characteristics of the children who live there. There will, however, be some consistency in the level of social and behavioural difficulty.

Generally they had entered care for the first time as teenagers because they could not get on with their families–only a third had done so before the age of eleven. A minority had been abused or had got into trouble outside the home. They were regarded as too difficult or too unwilling to be fostered; only a few had entered their current placement as part of a planned move. For around a third, the purposes of the placement were essentially short-term–to permit an assessment, to create a breathing space while plans were sorted out or to give the young person and his or her family a break from each other. For nearly half, there was another more ambitious, but nevertheless limited objective–such as to treat behaviour or to prepare for a long-term placement or for independence. For a sizeable minority the intention was that they should remain in the home until such time as they ceased to be looked after.

Such a description ranges between several groups of children with contrasting needs, prompting a fairly obvious question, equally vital to the concerns of those purchasing services and those providing residential placements: which groups can be brought together under the same roof without risk of undermining the aims and objectives of the intervention? Put simply, there is a question of 'mix'.

No combination of children is ideal, but if staff know what kind of children they are being asked to support, neither should any mix of children prove beyond the capabilities of a well run residential centre. Bullock and colleagues found that secure units were able to cope with young people who had been convicted of rape alongside victims of sexual abuse. It was not an ideal combination but it was nevertheless manageable. Whitaker and colleagues sum up the situation well when they say some combinations present staff with few difficulties but many opportunities, whereas others present few opportunities and many difficulties. They found that the quality of the combination depended on the balance of strengths and vulnerabilities among those whom the home sheltered: the stresses associated with looking after those in greater difficulty were moderated by the demands of the less taxing.

However, the consequences of getting the equation wrong can be serious indeed. Seven of the 36 children who had been sexually abused in the Bristol study subsequently sexually mistreated other children where they were living–three of them in residential placements–as did three of the 17 who had previously sexually abused another child. It is vital in this context that carers–including residential workers–understand the risks they are coping with and it may be that certain placements should be prepared specially for the most complex cases.

★ 3

Many of the studies identify gaps in knowledge about tackling children's problems. And where knowledge exists there can be a lack of necessary skill. It is not just a matter of controlling children whose behaviour is unacceptable, but of making judgements about the connections embedded in troublesome behaviour (if not of its causes) and of fashioning effective strategies to break chains of negative effects.

Information about individual children can be aggregated to establish a picture in a single home, an area within a social services department or across an entire local and health authority. Policies and practice with regard to improving patterns of social and behavioural difficulty should reflect such evidence. This strategy might extend not only to placement decisions (which types of children go where) but to the response appropriate for meeting challenges to professional competence.

★ 4

Too often, social workers in the field are forced to set the priority of finding a child an empty bed above any hope of finding a placement that will meet a child's needs. Too often, residential homes–especially superficially successful ones–are forced to admit ever more difficult children, whose needs are increasingly likely to be incompatible.

Information on children in need, particularly those looked after away from home, should be used to ensure a workable fit between children placed in the same setting.

The homes

A proportion of children in need will spend part of their lives in residential homes. On any day in 1996 about 8,000 children lived in 1,200 centres. Two-thirds of the places are currently managed by local authorities, which, according to the available evidence, do the job no better and no worse than the private and voluntary sector who provide the other third in roughly equal proportions. The growth of the private sector represents a significant change since 1985 when it was a less significant aspect of Berridge's research. Sinclair and Gibbs have made a special study of the private sector as part of this programme.

Most residential homes for children are unremarkable to look at. Even specialist secure centres for the most difficult and disturbed attract little public interest when they are run by local authorities. There are a few exceptions still–for example, the large therapeutic community based in an Adam mansion which was studied by Little and Kelly–but most modern homes are small. The York effectiveness study found that nearly half (48%) of the 48 they looked at had fewer than seven beds; and that four-fifths (82%) accommodated fewer than nine residents. The biggest home studied by any team sheltered only 20 children (although occasionally several small units shared a campus). These simple observations were found to have important implications for the management, cost and integration of residential care.

In nearly all 130 placements involved in the investigations discussed here, there were more staff than residents and roughly two-thirds of the staff were primarily involved in the social care of the children. (As Berridge and Brodie point out, this represents an increase in resources when compared with the situation a decade ago.) Staff-resident ratios are rather freely bandied about in social work: Sinclair and Gibbs used a different, more meaningful measure of the relationship–the average number of working hours per resident per week. It was found to be 61

★ 5

There is nothing in the overview studies to suggest that bigger homes do any better than smaller ones. Results on staff to child ratios are more equivocal but it seems safe to conclude that adding more and more staff is not a recipe for success. Of course, the children in question require much more support than most, but expecting children to form many new relationships–especially when stays are short–can be counterproductive. There is also a critical balance to be struck between investment in the lives of the children while they are resident and once they get home or begin to live independently.

On the whole, it is better to keep the size of children's homes small and the ratio of staff to residents as low as possible. Such an arrangement will have the effect of reducing the costs of residence. Any savings would be wisely invested in providing children with services, for example support with housing, education or employment after they leave.

Types of residence

Residential care is a term that now encapsulates a wide array of services. Consider the following examples from the studies included in the overview.

Berridge and Brodie A home with two male and two female residents aged between 13 and 16, located on a main road in a busy urban area. Its purpose was described as providing short-term emergency care to permit planning for return home or transfer to an alternative placement.

Bullock and colleagues A specialist treatment centre sheltering 30 extremely difficult and disturbed young people in three secure units. Built in the 1960s and located on the edge of a middle-class neighbourhood in a commuter town. The security was not immediately apparent to the visitor.

Whitaker and colleagues A home for seven teenagers located on a main arterial road 20 minutes by bus from the centre of a large city. It was in a built-up area with several local shops nearby. The house itself was Victorian and obviously not purpose built. It was pleasantly furnished.

Berridge and Brodie A private home in a terrace house in an attractive street in Inner London. It provided therapeutic services for four young people for whom local authorities had no provision of their own.

Sinclair and Gibbs A large detached house in a long road of similar red brick buildings; easily missed when driving by. Well decorated with lots of pictures and ornaments.

hours on average for the 48 homes but one returned a figure of 141 hours. In the voluntary sector the ratio can be higher still.

Residence used to be equated with the notion of an institution and whatever else it stood for, an institution meant stability. Modern residence is more fluid; even the physical environment of placements can fluctuate. For example, one of the nine homes studied by Brown and colleagues changed location and several of the other investigations recount the rapid deterioration in the fabric of unhappy children's homes. There is the turnover of staff and residents also to be reckoned with. In the least stable of the homes, there were 17 arrivals or departures during a single month, compared with two changes in a year in the most stable. Next to be taken into account are alterations in the aims and objectives of residential centres, which are nowadays enshrined in statements of purpose and function.

The York study of cultures charted patterns of change in the homes with which they had contact. Some had improved markedly after a prolonged bad patch. Continued ups and downs were commonly viewed as an inevitable consequence of the changing mix of children. Some had been thrown out of equilibrium by a bad turn of events leading to vicissitudes which never reached crisis proportions. Others had persistent difficulty with only minor and unsustained upturns. At worst, homes suffered problems which triggered further difficulties which spiralled downwards out of control. As in this example:

> A home for six teenagers, mostly boys, admitted a 13-year-old about whom staff knew little. Subsequently, an 11-year-old victim of sexual abuse also became resident. Both boys repeatedly accused older residents of bullying them and after incidents which led to the 13-year-old being taken to the accident and emergency unit of the local hospital, two older boys were removed. The two younger boys were suspended from school for misbehaviour. They 'shopped' one of the other residents for selling drugs and became involved in delinquency themselves. The older of the two was accused of making a local girl pregnant and was moved to another home until the accusation was disproved. Staff began to leave due to stress. Control deteriorated. Fires were started and windows broken. Neighbours complained that the boys had falsely accused them of using drugs. In the end all the boys were moved and the home temporarily closed.

Change is not intrinsically bad. The studies describe homes that needed to change but remained much the same and good homes that experienced unhelpful development. The important thing is to know when change is required, how it is to be managed and what it is intended to achieve.

In the midst of change there is a danger that the children will drift. Clear aims and objectives for a home and its residents are necessary preconditions for effective residence. (This point is discussed further on page 49.) Objectives should extend to the fundamental right of any child to dignity and protection from harm. Not all homes have succeeded in meeting these basic requirements and children have suffered as a result.

★ 6

Residential centres for children are much more fluid environments than is commonly acknowledged and a high level of change is not always a negative factor. Children stay for much shorter periods than a decade ago and staff turnover remains high. The level of difficulty also appears to have risen in the sense that homes are frequently faced with new problems or new combinations of problems.

Frequent change in children's homes must be expected and ought to be better anticipated. The most reliable basis for forming judgements about a home is repeated assessment undertaken in collaboration with staff (and residents). If a home is considered to have hit a prolonged bad patch or to be caught in a downward spiral, external managers, heads of homes and service purchasers, as well as staff and residents, should try to work together to tackle the factors that have contributed to the downturn.

Sinclair and Gibbs found that two-fifths (44%) of children they talked to had been bullied during their stay and that one in seven (14%) had been taken advantage of sexually. In this context it is important to bear in mind Farmer and Pollock's finding that children, not just adults, instigate such abuse. As a consequence children become even unhappier than they were prior to being looked after. The York effectiveness study found that two-thirds of residents had been miserable or unhappy in the month prior to interview and that nearly two-fifths had contemplated suicide. Those who reported attempted bullying or sexual abuse within the home were much more likely to be miserable. On the other hand, those who were involved in work of some sort or who were proud of something they had done in their leisure time–activities common in stable, forward-looking children's homes–were usually happier.

If it is important for children's safety and simple happiness that they should avoid drift and find stability or a basis for ordered development, what can be done to encourage homes to create the right conditions? A number of possibilities exist. Many observers focus on organisational and political arrangements; others have sought solutions in the quality of the regime, that is to say in theoretical approaches to the treatment of troubled children. Then there is the day-to-day management of the home to be taken into account.

The way residential homes are organised into the continuum of personal services is a significant factor–it is discussed in greater depth in later sections–but as Whipp and colleagues demonstrate, there is no optimal arrangement. The width of the split between purchaser and provider will not in itself determine the effectiveness of homes, although it is important to have well thought out approaches to this aspect of the work. It is probably the case, however, that frequent changes in organisation are counter-productive: Berridge and Brodie, for instance, found staff were confused by the rapidly changing complexion of local and health authorities.

Which are better–private or public sector homes?

Today, some services for children in need–day services, foster care and residential placements–are provided by the private sector. Whether this change has been for the better is rather unclear as far as residential care is concerned. Private homes tend to be distant from the child's community, disconnected from other local and health authority supports and more likely to provide education on the premises. The York effectiveness study suggests, nevertheless, that remoteness reduces some of the pressures on children: for example, the lures of alcohol and glue-sniffing which can be an everyday preoccupation on inner city estates. Separation can also make clarity of purpose and staff cohesion–which emerge as ingredients vital to good outcomes–easier to achieve. Differences in the type of provision offered by the private and public sector might provoke greater discussion about the terms used. 'Private', of course, implies a willingness to make a living out of caring for children. The empirical evidence would also suggest that it has come to mean meeting public responsibility in a private context.

Predicting children's happiness

Sinclair and Gibbs arrived at a measure of well-being by adding together scores from several variables and deducing what combination of factors seemed broadly to correspond with the notion of a happy resident. What happens in the home, particularly bullying and maltreatment, are significant influences. They also found that gender made a difference: boys tended to be happier than girls; having a friend or a group of friends and wanting to be in residential care were also powerful predictors of general happiness. Social work activity, on the other hand, did not seem to bear very strongly on the outcome.

In the quest for a reasonably high quality of care, local and health authorities, particularly those in the smaller London boroughs, have turned increasingly to the private sector. Evidence from Sinclair and Gibbs suggests that private homes do a different job from those in the public sector, mainly looking after very difficult children in placements at some distance from the the children's families. Most undertake the task very successfully.

The preoccupation with treatment regime has also led into a blind alley. Dartington's studies of the more difficult children found that certain approaches suited some groups of children but not others: no single programme was suitable in all cases. Generally speaking, treatment approaches which encourage a young person to understand how the family contributed to the pathology and which involve the family in that process are more likely to have some beneficial effect. However, this general proposition tends to hold truer in particular contexts–such as specialist treatment centres–than in the more ordinary run of children's homes.

This evidence suggests that sweeping pronouncements about the organisation of residence or the theoretical approach are of limited value in terms of securing stability or ordered development within an individual home. (This is not to say that organisation or theoretical approaches are unimportant.) Avoiding drift has to be the priority, and that cannot be guaranteed by pronouncement from the centre alone.

Results from the York effectiveness and Luton studies show that children's homes were more easily kept in reasonably good shape if they were small; if the head of home felt that its functions were clear, mutually compatible and not disturbed by reorganisation; if the head of home was given adequate autonomy and if the staff agreed on how the home should be run and were not otherwise at odds with each other.

These findings, Sinclair and Gibbs suggest, can be reduced to a simpler equation. The problem, as they see it, is to get the residents to agree on what is acceptable behaviour; the solution is to establish small homes in which staff and management can reach a consensus about aims and objectives.

These findings tend to emphasise the importance of the contribution to the wider scheme of things of the head of home and the staff. It must, of course, be true that a good head of home, like a good headteacher or an effective middle manager, will run a better organisation than a poor one, and it is therefore vital that a manager's performance is regularly reviewed. But it is as important to the well-being of residential homes in general to know what a good manager *does* as it is to know who the good managers are.

As the concluding sections of this overview demonstrate, effective managers tend to focus first on the aims and objectives of residence. If they are coherent, there tends to be a healthy culture, meaning that staff and residents will broadly agree on how to respond both to routine and more difficult tasks in the home. When clear objectives produce a healthy culture, residents tend to be happier and outcomes tend to improve.

★ 7

Experienced managers and professionals in the personal social services have long since given up the quest for a holy grail of treatment. It is certainly unlikely that either behaviour modification or psychotherapy alone has the answer. Outcomes for children looked after are usually explained by a combination of factors: the child's background, taking into account the prognosis were no intervention to be attempted; the services provided on behalf of the child and his or her family, with special attention to the match between needs and services, and any protective factors operating in the child's favour.

Treatment regimes should be seen in the context of the child's background and prognosis. Residents in children's homes, generally speaking, do not have needs that demand specialist treatment approaches within the home itself; their needs may, on the other hand, require support from outside professionals.

★ 8

Being clear about the objectives of a children's home is essential to the success of a children's home. A good head of home will work from (and in some cases be responsible for establishing) these objectives and ensure that they are met.

The ingredients of high quality residential care extend to appointment procedures and support mechanisms for heads of homes. Some people appointed as heads of home will not take to the job. Monitoring a manager's performance and offering support when difficulties occur should be integral to the management structure. Replacement managers with a track record of turning around failing homes will continue to be a valuable asset.

Staff and their tasks

It should go without saying that staff are an essential ingredient of successful residence. Who is recruited, what they are asked to do, how equipped they are to respond, how they cope with stress, how well they work with each other as well as with professionals outside of the home– all these factors will come to bear on their practice and, as a consequence, on the well-being of the residents.

Three-fifths of the children in residential placements are male, three-fifths of the staff are female. Approximately one staff member in ten is from a minority ethnic group, nearly all of African or African-Caribbean descent–about the same proportion as the children. The average age of staff members is about 40, although a fifth are aged under 30 and about 15% over 50. About two-fifths are part-time and the majority have at least two years experience. About 10% of the residential workforce are designated as having domestic tasks connected with cooking, cleaning or keeping watch at night. Some seven per cent are called Unit Managers. The remainder have some caring role, which, for 13%, will be combined with day to day social work.

Comparing the situation with that in 1985, Berridge and Brodie found that there are now more staff with more experience of residential work although it will frequently have been gathered across several settings. There are more men employed in the sector than there were a decade ago and, although there is no reliable equivalent data, it seems safe to conclude that there are now more staff from minority ethnic groups. Farmer and Pollock give the characteristics of residential staff and foster parents supporting sexually abused or abusing children: there is little to distinguish between the two adult groups.

★ 9

Residential staff have broad ranging responsibilities, as the findings outlined on the left indicate. It is important, therefore, to have mechanisms that encourage staff to keep sight of their principal responsibility, the priorities for the child and the home and the division of labour with other professionals. This will contribute not only to the well being of the home and its residents but will also enable staff to maintain realistic career aspirations.

★ 10

Terms and conditions for residential staff should extend to their authority and autonomy to influence decisions concerning children in their care. Career reviews might usefully set out what staff are able and permitted to do at successive stages of their career, and what skills will be needed before greater authority and autonomy can be assumed.

The hybrid nature of the job

The studies dealing with the residential experience demonstrate how children looked after benefit from a mixture of what might be called ordinary parenting and specialist help. Whitaker and colleagues give a series of examples of direct work with residents which illustrates the hybrid nature of the job. The following is typical.

Helping a boy of 11 to have a satisfying life
Jack could not read. He was reasonably well behaved and had not yet reached puberty. He wanted to be in the children's home and enjoyed school. He was liked by the other residents, most of whom were older than him. The staff sought to make Jack's life happy while helping him with his learning disability. They talked to him about his school day, provided reassurance when needed, showed appreciation for his achievements and gave him tasks to do in the home. This helped his development, for instance in handling and making good use of money.

What residential workers think they are good at

The York effectiveness study asked residential social workers about their job as it was and how they would like it to be. In relation to the following activities, there was satisfaction: in the main, those who wanted to be involved with them were involved, and those who did not were not.
   domestic tasks
   administration
   keeping order and supervision
   showing concern for young people
   social training
   acting as a key or primary worker.
In relation to the following areas of work, considerably more staff said they felt they ought to be involved than actually were:
   education
   work training
   care planning
   contact with families
   after care
   therapeutic work
   staff supervision and leadership.
The latter tasks more often involved people outside the home.

The York study of cultures summarises the tasks of a residential worker. Some of the day is spent supporting individual residents. Part of the job, naturally, involves working with the group of children living in the home. Other aspects will include collaborating with other professionals, with the social worker supporting the family and possibly with specialist health or education practitioners. Beyond that there will be the children's family and home networks, including school, to attend to. And, more important, if all the other tasks are to be completed satisfactorily, staff must be able to maintain a cohesive team approach.

Within these categories, the range of potential activity can be bewildering. Whitaker and colleagues set out a list of problems staff face. They include identifying and stopping bullying, ensuring that residents do not manipulate each other to misbehave, discouraging residents from running away and/or offending or causing damage to the home or its environs, monitoring the emotional and sexual relationship of residents and preventing sexual abuse. The list is by no means comprehensive but it suffices to illustrate the range of possibilities a residential worker might anticipate on the way to work each day.

As with most jobs, there are attendant stresses. Ensuring residents receive adequate individual attention is emotionally draining. Being hit or verbally abused by young people also takes its toll. But the greatest drain on the resources of residential staff occurs when they feel unable to control events around them. Several studies record staff disquiet at not having a say over who is admitted to a home, at being uncertain about the differential risks posed by residents (individually and collectively) and at lacking the skills to deal with recurrent problems. Whitaker and colleagues describe how stresses can accumulate to undermine the practice of even the most proficient staff team.

Sinclair and Gibbs approached the question of staff authority and autonomy from a different direction. They asked residential workers about various aspects of their job, as it existed and how they would like it to be. Nearly all of the areas of dissatisfaction hinged on life outside the home: for example, concerns about the child's education, his or her relationships with relatives and progress after leaving residence. Residential workers' sense of being cut off from the other services provided on the child's behalf is apparent in several of the studies.

THE MANAGEMENT OF PERSONAL AND SEXUAL RELATIONSHIPS

Society is understandably preoccupied with revelations about the abuse residential staff may have inflicted on children, even when the abuses occurred as long as two or more decades ago. The concern is to ensure that such apparently widespread maltreatment is never repeated. Among today's generation of care staff, however, the preoccupations have less to do with the quality of relations between adults and children than with those between child and child. The evidence from the studies supports this assessment of current risk. Seven of the 40 children in the Bristol study had sexually abused another child while in foster and/or residential homes; nearly a quarter (23%) of the girls and seven per cent of the boys

★ II

Damaging stress levels can be reduced if staff feel they can influence their own destiny. They will feel more in control if there is a free flow of appropriate information. Where information is lost or unnecessarily restricted, morale frequently suffers, rumours abound and mistrust and conflict among staff members often follow.

Effective channels of communication in residential homes will enable the staff to do their job well. Managers need to be kept informed about what staff discover in their day to day involvement with the children; front line workers need to keep up to date with a manager's strategic thinking. Communication should go beyond the directives and guidelines that are sometimes a feature of less forward looking homes.

★ 12

The importance of matching children's multiple needs with a continuum of services is a recurring theme in these pages. Residential care may provide a part of the right response to the needs of troubled children but it is seldom adequate by itself; other social workers, health professionals, school and employment specialists may also have a role to play. Not only do these services have to be available, they must be organised so that they are part of a demonstrably coherent whole.

More management resources should be devoted to breaking down the isolation of residential services. Better communication will help, but it may also be necessary to improve the integration of services, for example through training, appraisal systems, joint working patterns and consultancy.

in the York effectiveness study said they had been taken advantage of sexually while resident.

Underlying the risk of actual maltreatment is the question of how ordinary behaviour among young people reaching puberty is to be managed. In many ways, physical maturity is the Achilles' heel of residence. Even in relatively untroubled families, parents will often struggle to come to terms with the emerging sexuality of their offspring. The demands of maintaining a professional relationship with several children caught in the tide of their sexual development can be overwhelming. What is more, for those working with adolescents, questions of sex are omnipresent but seldom offset by the compensations most parents have of seeing their children enter adulthood.

Four messages from research may help to clarify and improve practice. The first has been mentioned already. Ensuring that information is shared and placement decisions reflect a proper assessment of a child's needs is important. Knowledge about whether a child has been abused, whether there is any evidence of abusive behaviour, whether the maltreatment has left a clear pattern of symptoms–particularly when a reckoning is made of a child's age and normal sexual experiences–will help residential workers feel confident they are providing appropriate protection for children and are not overwhelmed by the management of sexual relationships.

★ 13

Where residential workers–or foster carers–are uncertain about what to expect in the sexual behaviour of the children in their care, it becomes difficult to set appropriate boundaries. There is a present tendency both to normalise behaviour which is potentially damaging to the child and to others and to treat as risky behaviour what ought to be treated as unremarkable adolescent behaviour.

Child protection services in local and health authorities could usefully introduce advice about the care of sexually abused and abusing children to policy and practice. It might include making specialists available whom residential workers could consult over difficult child management issues. Building up a knowledge base on the care and control of sexually abusing children could be regarded as part of the service.

Coping with sexual behaviour: ordinary relationships

The prevention of sexual abuse is, of course, a primary aim of children's services. The problem is how to disentangle maltreatment from behaviour that lies on the borderline of what might be called ordinary adolescent development. Where victims of sexual abuse or children who have abused others are in residential care, establishing clear thresholds for acceptable behaviour is even more difficult. Consider the following two, fairly typical scenarios from the York study of cultures.

A girl of 16 became sexually involved with a boy of 14. The staff felt the 14 year old was being exploited by this older, sexually experienced girl. Matters became worse when the 16 year old took up with another boy in the home, also younger. Conflict, envy and resentment spread.

and from a different home;

While several members of staff and a number of young people were on an outing at the seaside, a girl of 16, who often behaved in a sexually provocative way, suddenly peeled away from the group and began running across the sand. Four slightly younger boys immediately ran after her. All of them disappeared from view behind a building.

Coping with sexual behaviour: prostitution

The emphasis here is on the good management of ordinary sexual relations between young people since it is a source of so much stress to staff. But some much more extreme behaviour they might occasionally encounter would test the most experienced professional. Farmer and Pollock report on how children's homes and foster parents struggled to control five young people (one girl and four boys) who had become involved in prostitution. Professional attention is pulled in several directions at once: there is a natural desire to control the behaviour; there is a need to encourage health protection; there are the legal issues–some of these children are breaking the law; there is a concern to prosecute the men who pay for the sex and there is a need to protect other children who may be enticed into prostitution. The evidence from Farmer and Pollock indicates that professionals experience great difficulty in such circumstances. The behaviour of young people involved in prostitution may be as compulsive as is delinquency among persistent offenders, but far less is known about the aetiology, useful intervention strategies or likely prognoses. Presently, to put a distance between the young people and their network of clients and pimps seems to be the only strategy likely to succeed.

The second message is that residential workers should be equipped with the skills to interpret children's behaviour. Smith and colleagues reported in *Child Protection: Messages from Research* that two-thirds of ordinary parents had seen their child masturbating. It is essential that practitioners are able to distinguish abnormal behaviour from the ordinary when deciding if and when to intervene. As Farmer and Pollock demonstrate, it is also important that the interpretation of behaviour by staff is not hidebound by gender stereotypes: male to female sexual advances may be more likely to be considered abusive than female to male and high levels of sexual activity are commonly thought to be less appropriate among girls. At the other extreme, there are some incontravertibly dangerous behaviours about which relatively little is known. The Bristol researchers, for example, report on the problems of supporting sexualised adolescent girls, young people involved in prostitution–boys as well as girls–and young abusers. These sub-groups of children were hardly acknowledged by the care system even a decade ago.

The third and fourth messages concern opportunities for good general practice that may be overlooked in the hubbub of a residential home under pressure. Being clear about what kind of behaviour is acceptable and what is not and establishing boundaries that can be explained and enforced are pivotal to good relations in any children's home.

Rules and sanctions have a much better chance of success if the rationale behind them is also explicit. Curiously, in many residential centres, which because of the age and other characteristics of the young people they shelter are liable to be hothouses of sexual activity, there is often a distinct reluctance to talk about sex or to tolerate any display of affection or sexual interest. An openness to discussion extending to education about relationships and sex and other training is shown by the studies to be a far more effective strategy.

CULTURE AND MORALE

Culture is a word much used by those who have studied institutions. It seldom refers to questions about the value of the arts, which is a subject usually overlooked altogether, but to some of the less easily defined aspects of residence: the ambience, the general sense of well-being, the relationship between the people–all of which may hold clues to good practice. As the conclusion to this book will indicate, culture is fundamental to good outcomes, and so an attempt has been made in the closing pages to indicate how it can be manipulated to achieve good results on behalf of children.

When a group of people work or live together, a culture evolves: it is something greater than the sum of the behaviour, attitudes and aspirations of the individuals. A group can also have a collective morale. Some homes can remain cheerful when one or two of the individuals within are unhappy; elsewhere a general pessimism may ruin any prospect of harmless fun. Given the stresses and problems encountered by staff, it would seem reasonable to expect the culture of a residential home to be

★ 14

Ordinary sexual experimentation is difficult to control. Young people living together in groups are as likely to form sexual relations with each other as young people in the same school or the same work place. By the same token, residential homes are good contexts in which to advise young people about the norms and risks of sexual behaviour, to prevent unwanted pregnancy, reduce health problems and promote social responsibility to each other.

Education about sexual behaviour and health can contribute to the reduction of management problems in residential settings and to better outcomes beyond them. Levels of unplanned pregnancies can be counted as one such outcome.

generally undermining and for morale frequently to be low. The studies that dealt with such questions each used slightly different measures but the findings support similar, rather less predictable conclusions.

The Luton researchers who monitored morale during the time they were living in the children's homes found no correlation between the degree of collective happiness and the specific circumstances of the residents. In other words, a home might smile through an encounter with seemingly insuperable difficulties and, conversely, low morale was found in apparently quite peaceful environments.

Sinclair and Gibbs equated morale with a combined score based on job satisfaction and found wide variation between the 48 homes they studied. Staff whose morale was high tended to have regular supervision as well as a role that extended to care planning, after care, contact with families and counselling. The unqualified novice usually appeared to be happier than the qualified and long employed, indicating–as many commentators have suggested before–a susceptibility to 'burnout'. Some homes have recognised the pattern to the extent of deliberately employing young graduates who may stay for a few years while they decide on their career. It was a feature of the voluntary home studied by Little and Kelly.

A rather similar research approach was taken with respect to the culture of the homes, and, as in the case of morale, quite different avenues of enquiry produced consistent results. Whitaker and colleagues focused on group dynamics and the way staff and residents coalesced or fragmented when they were in contact with other groups of professionals or managers or needed to respond to legislative edict. It was apparent, for example, that tensions around issues that threatened a home's well-being

Tests of morale and culture

Each of the studies goes into the questions of morale and culture in much more detail. The York effectiveness study found that job problems and the clarity with which the job was defined to be strongly associated to good morale. Those with the role of 'keyworker' - bringing high involvement in care planning, contact with families, after care, therapeutic work and a particular involvement with one or two residents from the wider group - also seemed to be more contented with their lot.

Brown and colleagues asked simple questions of staff tasks and roles to see how they responded:

- A new child arrives at the home
- A parent visits his or her child at the home
- A child behaves in a way that necessitates restraint
- A child refuses to go to school
- A child wets the bed.

A collective and positive response to common problems was generally good for the residents. Simply reflecting now and then on what to do in different situations can be good for morale and have the effect of pulling staff together.

could generate a sense of collective responsibility: if a child was excluded from school, ordinarily fractious staff might sometimes rediscover an *esprit de corps*.

While acknowledging the difficulties of measuring a culture, Brown and colleagues distilled the issues to a string of simple questions about staff and residents' responses to common tasks and problems. When a parent visited a home or a child ran away, did the staff respond intuitively as a group? How did children behave when there was a fight between residents? Did they behave alike–so suggesting a cultural response–or did they all do their own thing?

By these admittedly rather basic criteria, clear cultural patterns within ordinary children's homes were charted. Strong staff cultures were found in five of the nine homes studied by Brown and colleagues; in four of the five the effect on outcomes was positive, in the fifth it was negative. Had this Dartington study been mounted two or more decades ago when institutions were larger, an attempt would have been made to capture the child culture–on the basis that it had been previously hypothesised that a fragmented child culture was to be taken as a positive sign. The detail of these findings is less important than the theory that evolved around them. The culture inside residential centres is an ingredient of good outcomes. Getting staff to agree on certain tasks is likely to produce a healthy home, which in turn will produce better results for the residents. But culture is as much the product of other factors, the most important of which is the clarity of the aims and objectives for each residential centre, and clear aims and objectives are themselves only part of the pattern since they evolve most readily when there is some assuredness about the needs of the children being supported. Consequently the research suggests strongly that regular attention should be paid to the culture within residence, but that such attention does not begin with the cultural aspects of residence. The strength of the argument is tested further in the closing pages.

★ 15

The adage 'a trouble shared is a trouble halved' may have some relevance for residential work. Evidence from the studies certainly creates the impression that when the staff group is divided its troubles are likely to be doubled.

It seems sensible to monitor the cultural response of the home, for example by using the tools in 'True for Us' Exercise 8. It is also recommended that homes do those things (for example joint training and development) that ensure that the staff group is likely to be united and avoid those things (change of function, joining two teams, frequent use of temporary staff) which tend to be disruptive. Agreeing common policies and reactions in relation to bullying and sexual harassment might be a priority given the evidence described above.

Management, inspection and training

It is a key-stone of the arguments presented here that residential care is best seen in the wider context of children's lives and children's services. Whatever their circumstances, children will have links of some description with home, neighbourhood, school or work. Residential services have connections, too, for example with other interventions and safeguards, with health and education services and other activity undertaken by social workers. Administrative networks have also to be reckoned with. Staff have to be recruited for work in residential homes and their services have to be paid for, and so all must answer to others inside social services departments. Departments are in turn accountable to elected members and–for some of their functions–to central government. The interdisciplinary meeting of professional minds in social work also requires an organisational structure and implies some accountability. None of these connections is spontaneous or self sustaining: all have to be engineered and maintained.

Whipp and colleagues at Cardiff who concentrated on this area concluded that the management of residential services has to be understood in the context of a professional bureaucracy. They found that looked after children come to rely on several professional groups, each of which is largely independent, self-organised and trained outside the agency for which they work. Despite the sense of powerlessness expressed to researchers by many residential workers, practitioners actually enjoy a high degree of autonomy in their work. Furthermore, despite the aspiration to flexible structures designed round the needs of children, hierarchies in professional bureaucracies such as social services departments are as likely to reflect professional status as organisational chains of command.

There are many more mechanisms for managing public sector services than there is space here to describe them. Five have been chosen from those picked out by the research teams to illustrate principal themes:

- line management
- inspection and regulation
- training
- strategic planning
- the marshalling of available resources.

The predicament of modern management

The management of any organisation will generate tensions among staff from time to time. In the personal social services ordinary anxieties have been aggravated since the 1970s by a combination of rapid expansion and frequent change, which has made staff sceptical of the benefits of both. Nevertheless, further development of the residential sector is a theme running through this book, and it implies paying renewed attention to management arrangements, which, even in a medium-sized social services department, will encompass as many as 3,000 staff.

LINE MANAGEMENT

In a professional bureaucracy line managers often perform contradictory functions. In recent years, social services policy has emphasised control, ensuring that practitioners follow predefined guidelines. The line manager has to implement the guidance and at the same time to respect professional autonomy. Whipp and colleagues found considerable variation in the way local authorities asked line managers to go about their work, some giving them a specialist focus, others requiring them to oversee several areas and functions.

The Cardiff team took an inclusive view of management by considering a broad range of staff relationships, not just those determined by their line management responsibilities. Managers who organised in a collegial way–encouraging trust and leaving it to staff and residents to find solutions to apparent problems–seemed to have better success than those who were bureaucratic to the extent of insisting on the strict interpretation of rules and regulations. Much of the difference can be attributed to variations in management style: better to adopt a 'hands on' approach, to be inside the home helping out, than 'hands off', trying to maintain effective control from afar. Some managers were hampered simply by the extent of their responsibilities: those who understood the value of personal involvement but who managed as many as seven placements were bound to struggle. Prior residential experience helped some managers to do their job, but it was not an essential prerequisite.

Sinclair and Gibbs, whose findings emphasise the benefits good leadership can bring to residence, discuss what heads of homes can do in conjunction with other managers to ensure that the network of connections works effectively. Agreement between the head of home and those both above and below in the hierarchy is a crucial factor. Ideally, the agreement should encompass broad objectives and narrow concerns about how to handle a specific problem. It might also include aspects of the organisation itself, for example protecting staff and residents against the corrosive effects of reorganisation.

Managing for effectiveness

Whitaker and colleagues set out what managers do that promotes effective residence:
- they are clear about the needs of children being sheltered (and avoid unhelpful stereotypes)
- they keep in touch with the problems staff face (and do not trivialise apparently small difficulties)
- they support individual members of staff who have experienced particular difficulty (without detracting from the general running of the home)
- they seek to increase the standing and station of workers by eliciting and communicating their opinions (and avoiding rules of thumb held about the residential task)
- they ensure that homes are not forced to accept children whom they are ill-equipped to help (and are clear about who the home can effectively support)
- they keep staff up to date about developments at central and local government level (and avoid seeing all change as negative).

INSPECTION AND REGULATION

The management infrastructure on which services for children in need rests has to be checked to ensure it is functioning effectively. A host of inspection and regulation procedures are in place, many governed by the central and regional arms of the Social Services Inspectorate. Local and health authorities also have their own machinery and placements themselves have procedures for reviewing progress. Where education is provided, OFSTED–independent inspectors–will also be involved. Coordination appears to be lacking, however: there is little evidence in the studies to suggest much connection between these various levels of inspection, nor do inspections follow a regular pattern. Cardiff examined the regulatory requirement for children's homes to be visited monthly and reports presented to elected members. They tended to be observed as a ritual rather than an opportunity for development. There was no standard method and few authorities sought to encourage consistency to the small extent of employing a single individual to do the work. Opinions about the purpose of the inspections varied, too. Problems caused by mutual ignorance and the distance between inspectors and inspected were all too evident.

Just as there are different styles of line management so there are varying attitudes to inspection among local authorities. Whipp and colleagues contrast those local authorities who were determined merely to secure compliance with a central order with others who saw it as an opportunity for development. Achieving a measure of trust between the different aspects of the organisation that surround residence seems to be as important as achieving trust among those who live and work inside them.

TRAINING

Ensuring that staff have the right skills for their work is another way to connect residence to the social fabric to which it seeks to make a contribution. It is well known that few residential staff have any specialist qualifications. Some have university degrees–probably no more or less than the proportion to be found for the adult population as a whole–but few have degrees or any other qualification that implies knowledge appropriate to work with children in residential contexts. All the studies shed some light on this issue. Berridge and Brodie had the advantage of being able to compare the current situation with that of a decade ago. They found that more staff had qualifications but that only one in six had completed a social work course. Even in-service training was restricted to about two-fifths of staff and a significant minority (between 28 and 42%) received no training at all.

The York effectiveness study sought to answer the question, 'Does having a higher proportion of trained staff lead to better residence?' and, rather startling at first acquaintance, found that it did not. A useful secondary question might have been, 'What are the training needs of staff working with different groups of children in need?' (one that might benefit from further study). Knowing that the proportion of trained staff

★ 16

The degree of separation between residence and other personal social services is frequently mirrored in inspection and regulation procedures. Too often, inspection is something done to residence by someone else, who in perception, if not in fact, knows little about the residential scene. When inspections become disconnected from one another, residential centres are more likely to sense attack than to recognise potential support.

Shifting the balance from inspection towards procedures that encourage the continuous improvement of services could be a more effective route to better quality and value. Effective monitoring and regulation are as likely to be achieved through good supervision, better training and good use of management information as through the attentions of a detached regulatory framework. Such a shift might also save resources that could be reinvested in homes experiencing short-term difficulty.

is not an indicator of a good home, is not to deny the value of better training–rather the contrary, but it nevertheless seems safe to conclude that training is no panacaea.

The Tavistock team monitored a particular programme designed to increase the proportion of qualified staff in management positions in residence. Social work courses in eight sites were enhanced over a five year period to meet the needs of residential workers.

On the positive side, the initiative seemed to counterbalance the previously apparent loss of qualified staff from the residential sector. Tavistock also found that nearly nine out of ten (87%) of the staff who received the training went back to their work and that nearly two-thirds (64%) intended to stay in the sector for the foreseeable future. Those who left said they did so because of poor prospects, shift work and lack of autonomy. On the negative side, there was only anecdotal evidence that the homes the staff returned to were enhanced by their acquired experience or that looked after children benefited.

It seems clear that continually tinkering with conventional social work training in an attempt to meet the special requirements of residential care is unlikely to achieve very much. Nor will there be much to gain from setting up courses in isolation and trying to deal with each new crisis in turn. The different players on the residential field tend to disagree on this issue, but the research suggests that it would be better to be clear about the nature of the modern residential social work task before designing the appropriate training.

STRATEGIC PLANNING

It is unclear to what extent the considerable change in the use of residence in recent times has been planned. Homes have closed as part of a general movement in social care; but in the context of children's services the destination of those moved out of the sector has seldom been clear and some aspects of the trend have resembled an unruly retreat. In the midst of it all, evolving relationships inside and outside the social services structure have borne heavily on the residential context. Internally,

★ 17

Training is essentially a transmission of skills from the wise to the inexperienced. Over time, the endeavour may become obscured by bureaucracy, ritual or status. It is questionable whether the social work training of residential workers is as useful as it used to be and whether the skills transferred are relevant to the residential context or apply to other aspects of children's services.

Local authority training programmes could usefully be reviewed to determine the extent to which courses convey the skills of working with troubled children. Skills of this sort are likely to extend beyond the residential context, so making training an ideal vehicle for reconnecting residence with the wider world of the personal social services. Encouraging staff to assemble skills that are relevant across health, education and social services settings will improve the professional confidence of staff entering the residential sector.

A need for training strategies

The Cardiff team drew attention to the value of seeing training in relation to strategic approaches to personnel issues as well as the individual and professional requirements of the staff. The disconnection between these twin concerns has contributed to the dislocation of training from the broader child care policy issues described here.

The strengths of the new unitary authorities

The Cardiff team's study extended to the new unitary authorities established after the review of local government in the 1990s. The researchers were encouraged by what they found in the new agencies. More limited resources based on their smaller size have forced many to think afresh, particularly since there is little collective wisdom to fall back on about the children being served. A thorough review of needs has therefore been more common. Tribal hostilities between health, education and social services threaten survival under the new conditions so there has been much more in the way of inter-agency co-operation. Existing services are no longer assumed to be necessary and so there is greater likelihood of them being thoroughly reviewed.

relationships between children's homes and professionals placing children have increasingly been mediated by resource managers. Externally, as the strategic importance of children's homes has diminished, so contact with Health, Education and other special agencies has increased.

It is apparent from the research that there is a lack of information about children's needs and the likely demand on services that can usefully be incorporated in the strategic planning process. In fact, there is not much evidence that any effective strategic planning stems from a reliable picture of the circumstances of children in need. Change has been a result of other forces. As the Luton team point out, one consequence has been that residential workers and their managers say far more about the problems they face than about their accomplishments. This negative bias must weigh against the place of evidence in the strategic planning framework.

Were these deficiencies to be rooted in one local government department they might be more easily remedied. But they extend to Education and Health as well as to cross-agency groups, such as Youth Justice, all of whom have their own planning mechanisms. Since the volume of children going through residence has become relatively small compared to the volume of identified children in need, it is difficult for those providing services to make their voices heard in each of the relevant arenas.

THE MARSHALLING OF AVAILABLE RESOURCES

One obstacle to planning for residence is the problem of predicting the need for beds. It is difficult to establish how much residence is being used, what spare capacity exists and what alternative placements may be available. Run on hotel lines, children's homes ought to be full for as much of the time as is possible, but, as a service for specific groups of children in need, it makes better sense to run at 80% capacity for the sake of the few occasions when demand is unusually–but predictably– high. The absence of a technology to deal with this complication has meant homes have been packed with children who ought to have been placed elsewhere, while children who might have benefited from residence have been denied the opportunity.

Placement patterns–the length of children's stay, their likely call on different kinds of residential and foster care, the combination of other services they are likely to require–are predictable. But the information needed in order to make an accurate forecast is largely missing from the resource management process, except, as Whipp and colleagues point out, in the form of the legacy of previous practice, which may boil down to a prejudice against the intractability of certain children's problems and the value of certain services. Though they may be perceived as disorganised and unhelpful, predictably complicated patterns of placement can achieve good outcomes for certain groups of children.

Much of this adds up to a need to review ideas about efficiency in relation to residence. 'Full' may or may not equate with 'good' where homes are concerned. Staff to child ratios and the qualifications (and

★ 18

Giving staff skills to enable them to work flexibly across the personal social services is a desirable goal with obvious advantages where the difficulties of strategic planning are concerned. Training alone is not a sufficient remedy, however: the infrastructure of the personal social services also requires adjustment.

As the goal of a Part III continuum of services becomes a reality, the demand for a skilled, flexible workforce will increase. Policies that encourage working across contexts and treat staff as members of a team with competencies beyond the residential sector will be of general benefit.

★ 19

Too often, the management of resources takes the placement as its starting point, not the child or the wider set of administrative and professional services necessary to make the placement work. A few local authorities have begun to design their services around prominent groups of children in need. This may prove to be a fruitful area for development.

Policies, infrastructure, practice frameworks and training should be built around the needs of identified groups of children being looked after. Work that begins with those particularly at risk of poor outcomes–for example, highly sexualised adolescents–could provide local authorities with a route to this way of operating.

therefore salary) of different types of staff also warrant a second look. Depending on the circumstances, short stays may be counterproductive and long stays not always justified. It may help to reconsider these questions in the light of the current preoccupation with 'best value' (which implies a comparison between properly costed alternative services and the evidence of their respective benefits in terms of outcomes for children).

HOW LOCAL AUTHORITIES ARE ORGANISED

Line management, inspection, regulation, training, strategic planning and the marshalling of resources all function within local and health authority structures. Whipp and colleagues identified a variety of patterns inside social services departments. They discovered that some revolved around the functions of the department: to protect children, support families, look after children and so forth. Some were based on geography so that departments were separated north, east, west and south. Less common were structures that reflected the characteristics of the clients they served. Although most distinguished readily between adults and children, at the point of organising services they were more reluctant to distinguish for example between those with parenting problems, child behaviour problems, relationship problems and so on. Preparedness to acknowledge the purchasing and providing functions of a public sector agency increased in the 1980s but waned in the 1990s. Current trends are towards greater centralisation, specialisation and a closer tie between resources and an understanding of needs of the kind advocated in this publication.

The Cardiff team also identified a hybrid model of organisation and, in truth, all local authorities can be classified into this last group since functions, geography, client base and arrangements to find and provide service must all be acknowledged. As social services departments have evolved over the last 30 years, no single pattern has come to dominate or can be shown to have been the most effective, but certain features introduced into any organisational structure will have a significant impact.

The first is stability: a structure which allows professionals and consumers a sense of certainty about what will be happening in the foreseeable future. The second - at first sight contradictory - is flexibility: arrangements that encourage frequent reflection and adaptation to meet contemporary concerns. The third is receptiveness: consistent acknowledgement of the needs of the children and families being served and determination to look for management models that support professionals in their work .

★ 20

Sinclair and Gibbs found the proportion of trained staff made little appreciable difference to the quality of care provided. But residence has its skills and the Tavistock team found some benefits from an intensive programme to transfer these skills to new staff.

A general review of the training requirements of staff working with children in need might be timely. Rather than taking as a starting point a particular aspect of the personal social services, it may be more fruitful to consider the skills necessary to work with different groups of children in need. Training may also be necessary to facilitate the management of staff employed to meet children's needs. Training is better viewed in the context of lifelong learning than within the existing structures of social work training.

Residence in its wider context

Whatever their circumstances, children in modern societies accumulate relationships with state institutions as they grow up. These relationships will figure more prominently in the lives of children in need as a result of their greater dependence on specialist help. If children enter residential care their relationships will travel with them and they may require attention and maintenance just as much as their links with family and neighbourhood.

Residential centres have relationships of their own with wider society. Most local authority settings are near to the neighbourhoods in which the children they accommodate grow up and so there is the potential for the placement to forge connections with the community similar to that of any other household. Private homes, as Sinclair and Gibbs have shown, tend to be more remote from the neighbourhoods of children's families, requiring a rather different set of tactics to keep residents in touch with family and friends without causing annoyance to local people.

There has been an unfortunate tendency in the residential world to see the placement and not the child as the fulcrum of all these relationships. Connections are likely to be expressed in terms of professional lines of accountability–from key worker to field worker to family rather than from the child to family. This view is particularly unhelpful in contexts where residence is forced to be 'a place of last resort' or 'the end of the line'–descriptions all too common. Of course, some placements aspire to and excel in just that role, but generally such thinking tends to isolate residence when, in reality, all the children that come into an institutional context will eventually leave it and nowadays the departure often follows soon after entry.

Changing attitudes that regard residence as a darkened door at the end of the line seems a vital step towards reintegrating the residential services into the wider context of social care. Together with other interventions, residential care seeks to make a measurable improvement to the quality of a child's life compared to what would have been the likely situation had no intervention or a different intervention been offered. One must hope that professionals will soon come to take it for granted

★ 21

Planning for children in need too often pivots on administrative dates, such as the two year review, sixteenth or eighteenth birthdays or the end of a placement. The administrative pulse is seldom in time with the rhythms and continuities of a child's own life.

Children in need, especially those looked after, might be better served if professionals were to set out attainable outcomes in all aspects of a child's life in relation to a selection of moments that seemed meaningful to child and family alike. By asking, for example, where a child is likely to be living in two, five and ten years time; what the nature of family relationships is likely to be, and similar questions related to education, health and social relations, it should be possible to see how residence and other services can contribute to good outcomes–as distinct from considering what outcomes can be salvaged from the residential context.

★ 22

Residence often comes late in the sequence of events that leads to a child becoming in need of specialist help. But if the ideas set out to the left are taken on board, residential ministering can be viewed as 'early'.

Looking for signs of later difficulty in an adolescent's life can be viewed as 'early intervention'. Looking for signals pointing to running away, delinquency, drug misuse or significant relationship problems in the years that follow entry to care or accommodation are to be encouraged.

Leaving care and leaving home

Young people long in care or accommodation leave 'home' much earlier than young people ordinarily leave the family home. Biehal and colleagues found that a quarter moved on when aged just 16, sometimes because the placement broke down but too often because of the traditional expectations of a personal social services intervention. Little and Kelly echo the point when they chart the 'all' or 'nothing' attitudes of the long-stay therapeutic communities; 'all'–the assumption that the job can be done by residence alone and that there is no alternative to the therapeutic milieu, and 'nothing'–that certain young people who would not respond to treatment were rejected by the residential centre and were forced into situations where they received a fraction of the support they received in the placement.

that for most children the best way forward need not involve any intervention but that for a few residence will be an essential component of the solution. Residential workers need to consider not only who is working alongside them in the common cause but also how the different services will ebb and flow in the lives of the children later on.

Failure to see residence as part of a larger fabric or to take proper account of the network of relationships is likely to have damaging consequences. As well as prolonging the isolation of residential placements, outcomes for the children are likely to be worse. Two dimensions of their lives, education and running away behaviour, serve to illustrate the point.

EDUCATION

Since the mid 1980s, the educational deficits of children looked after have probably increased, as the findings reported below illustrate. An extra complication has been added to the relationship between a child's social and educational needs: today it is much more common for schools to exclude errant pupils, temporarily or permanently. Sinclair and Gibbs found that half (49%) of the children they surveyed were at school; 29% had left school but 12% were excluded (leaving nine per cent who were waiting for a new school). Thus, at the time of the study, nearly a third of school age children were not in full-time education. The Luton team, who note that refusal and irregular attendance are as much a problem as exclusion, found that only three of the 21 young people in the adolescent homes were regularly attending school. Sinclair and Gibbs came to the conclusion that boys and those who had experienced a previous foster home breakdown or who were troublesome outside the children's home were particularly vulnerable to losing educational opportunities; Farmer

★ 23

Much of the evidence in the research studies, coupled with information collected locally, will require agencies to reflect on their partnerships. Sinclair and Gibbs rated over a third (35%) of residents eligible for work as having little participation in employment. The figure indicates the likely benefit of better co-operation between social services departments and further education colleges, employers and welfare to work programmes. Almost a half of residents (46%) had low participation in school, suggesting, similarly, that education departments should reconsider their level of engagement with social services.

Children in need would benefit if local authorities were to specify a joint policy at all levels of the organisation concerning the relationship between social services and education departments. It should extend to educational advice and support for residential and foster homes looking after school age children. Similar cross-agency statements could enhance young people's employment chances.

Education then and now

Berridge and Brodie highlighted the education of children looked after as a weakness of services in 1985. In the late 1990s the situation had changed but not really for the better. Fewer residents in ordinary children's homes were now in mainstream schools (49% today; 80% in 1985). More were going to special schools (35% compared to 15%) and some 10% were being educated in private homes (there were none in the study a decade and a half ago). The majority (53%) surveyed by the Luton researchers—whose study was unique in that it included children with a disability—had a special educational need recognised by an educational psychologist. By any reckoning educational needs among most children living away from home are severe.

Running away, foster care and residence

The study by Wade and colleagues suggests that as many as one in seven children run away from their parental home. Comparisons with foster care have eluded accurate analysis but they consider the rate to be at least 1 in 20. Four in ten children in residence run away. The range in absenteeism varies markedly between local authorities, so much so that four of the 32 homes in the York researchers' study accommodated over two-fifths (42%) of those who went missing.

and Pollock concluded that sexually abused and abusing children were similarly disadvantaged.

A failure to engage children in Education will have an impact on the well-being of a home as well as the long-term progress of the children. The York leaving care studies found that two-thirds of the children they followed did not pass a GCSE and a similar proportion failed to establish a stable career pattern within the next two years. Bullock and colleagues, who on many fronts recorded some encouraging outcomes for the most difficult and disturbed adolescents, established that only a handful gained any qualifications. Half managed to find work during the two-year follow-up period, but half of those lost their jobs within three days of starting. Little and Kelly, who focused on a therapeutic community where there was a declared effort to excel in education found a much brighter prospect, suggesting that good school outcomes are possible even for the most severely disadvantaged pupils.

RUNNING AWAY AND MOVING ON

Children who are looked after are much more likely to run away from home than are less troubled children. Experience of abuse or neglect or simple unhappiness prompts a desire to escape. Many children who run away from foster homes or residential centres have also run away from the family home in the past. If these children are again visited with coercion, bullying or a sense of insecurity when they are being looked after–and the evidence retold in the previous pages suggest that they frequently are–then the urge to run away will be great indeed.

Wade and colleagues identified two patterns of running away. One group of children went to friends or family–usually friends–for fairly extensive periods and returned voluntarily. A second group ran away for shorter periods, were more likely to sleep rough, did not want to return and were prone to offend while away. The Bristol research acts as a reminder that young people involved in prostitution figure in this group.

How children move on from residence would seem a useful proxy measure for the contribution it makes to a child's long-term well being. Most children progress in a planned way. They will go to live with relatives or move to a subsequent stage in the continuum of services designed to meet their needs. But others, whose problems are much the same, suffer away from home much as they may have done while at home and so are prone to run, putting themselves at risk of greater difficulty. The alternative routes might be regarded as a metaphor for the future of residence itself. It may attend to its shortcomings and secure a valuable place for itself in the personal social services or, by neglecting the messages of research, contribute further to the continued unhappiness of a significant group of children.

★ 24

Wade and colleagues discovered that some local authorities had much higher rates of running away.

Directors of social services should know how many children they are looking after each night and where. By virtue of their characteristics, some of these children are likely to be missing temporarily and special concern will be expressed about their well being. It is not realistic to expect children never to run away. It is realistic to expect to know who is away, for how long, from where and why.

The York study of going missing begins to provide a technology to help predict which children looked after will run away. Local authorities can use information systems to improve this technology. Going missing should not be viewed simply as a failure to care: certain children looked after will always think of running away. Knowing which children are the more likely to run away, what can be done to prevent such an occurrence and which runaways are likely to put themselves at greatest risk of further harm will help to fashion more effective intervention.

Conclusions

This book began by sketching some of the hard realities and challenges facing residential care. The evidence just reviewed confirms the proposition of a set of services at a crossroads. More of the same simply will not do. Over the next five years, central and local government, managers of children's services and practitioners have difficult decisions to make about which children in need can benefit from residence, what can realistically be expected from the intervention and the relationship between this kind of care and anything else available from Health, Education or Social Services.

By the same token, it is an auspicious moment to consider development. The Government is reviewing spending on all public sector services and asking searching questions about which provision gives best value. Several Government departments have come together to consider a response to the report of Sir William Utting on the safety of children living away from home. The Association of Directors of Social Services has sought comment on a new vision for children's services: no Director is entirely happy with services for children living away from home, but few if any are prepared to countenance doing without residential services altogether.

Doubts about the value of residence have to be seen against a background of general uncertainty about how to help different groups of children in need. Commentators are beginning to acknowledge how little is known about the circumstances and prospects of the children whom residential services are meant to support.

Changing times, changing definitions

A definition of residential care for children looked after away from home is set out on page 7. The greater the accumulation of evidence, the less convincing the distinction between residential placements and other placements becomes. Typical features such as size, cost, length of stay and treatment nowadays count for less and less. In future, it may be more helpful to classify placements according to the following criteria:

- Do children in need live in the placement?
- What groups of children in need are accepted for placement?
- How many other children live in the placement?
- What services are provided within the placement?
- Do the carers live permanently in the placement?

The research evidence does not suggest any radically new intervention–at least not in the first instance; but it does indicate a need to establish a radically different environment in which those responsible for providing the wider range of services can respond to change and learn from their mistakes before implementing any further development. Residential contexts–children's homes, family centres, secure units and places of respite–are unusually well-suited to an enterprising climate where there is an acknowledged pursuit of best practice.

If such an environment could also engender greater certainty about what can reasonably be expected to be achieved on behalf of different groups of children in need, then progress would be more likely still. It is clear from the previous section that such children must not have to endure disruption, bullying and sexual harassment on so great a scale, but it is unrealistic to hope that they can be eliminated altogether, any more than any other causes of childhood unhappiness. There is great scope for improving the educational performance of children in residential care, but it is not realistic either to expect them all to excel. Children in need have problems, some of which defy our understanding. That is why some are placed in residential contexts. More realistic is an expectation of year-on-year improvement in services in each of the areas just described, supported by a good enough record of the sort of information that will permit practitioners and managers to assess how and why progress is being made.

If there is an appetite for radical change, it is not the job of this publication to say precisely what should be done, but it can indicate certain options that will support any timetable for development. The first two suggestions are essentially a restatement of what has been said already and so are described only briefly. The third suggests a framework within which the messages of the research discussed in this overview can be implemented.

The first way a local authority or a health authority could implement the messages of the research would be to act on the 24 recommendations for effective development set out in the margins of the preceding pages. Better communications, careful attention to the size of homes and to the staff-child ratio, the selection of good heads of homes, the application of best-value concepts to out-of-area placements and the monitoring of children's educational development–to summarise just five–will help to improve residence in any local authority. But to act on recommendations is not sufficient in itself to establish high quality services.

The second way a local authority or a health authority can implement the messages from the research would be to act upon factors associated with what several of the research teams came to call 'good homes'. The term was used most precisely in the York effectiveness study, which used robust methods to show that **small homes** run by somebody who has **a clear idea about what the home is trying to achieve and how to do it,** and encourages **contact with family members** while respecting the fact that many residents do not wish to live at home are the most likely to achieve good outcomes on behalf of children. Local authorities would do well to check every residential centre that takes in the children they look after against these criteria.

Sinclair and Gibbs used multi-variate analysis to isolate factors which in combination seemed to lead to the best result. Of course, there will always be exceptions: some big homes do well; not all good homes have good leaders; some short-stay and respite homes will prosper by ensuring children do not stay very long, but the results are important because they permit analysis of the components of a good service–but, again, it is not the whole story: a successful placement is more than the sum of its positive attributes.

Establishing the principles for effective development

- It is important to acknowledge the value of what exists. Few planners will ever have the luxury of a clean sheet to work on and most local authorities have plant and traditions that tend to restrict their aspirations.
- It is necessary to work within existing budgets. There is nothing in these pages to suggest services can be improved simply as a result of making more resources available but, in any case, the working assumption must be that public sector service spending will be tightly pegged. It is likely to be a matter of making more with what there is.
- Forward planning will need to make at least passing acknowledgement of the broad trends within the sector as a whole, for example, towards the better linking of prevention, early intervention, treatment and social prevention, to the concept of 'best value', to an improved evidence base and to a clearer link between identified needs and services.
- Within the range of possibilities, there will be areas of work which, by virtue of public concern, evidence or consumer demand, warrant a higher priority. Youth justice and adolescent mental health might be viewed in this light.
- A range of tools has been designed to enable policy makers, managers and clinicians to improve services. It is better to investigate what is available than to begin afresh.
- The best solutions on behalf of children in need almost always result from cross-agency co-operation .
- Any development should take into account the differing responsibilities of policy makers, managers and researchers–who tend to think about *groups* of children in need– and clinicians, social workers, health professionals and teachers–whose first thought is for the individual child.

The third way a local authority or a health authority can implement the messages from the research would be to establish a systematic framework within which change can be introduced, monitored and the results disseminated. The one suggested here is aimed at policy makers and/or managers of children's services. By definition, such a perspective implies readiness to take into account the responsibilities of residential workers. The starting point for them will be something like this: here are the services for which I am responsible; here are the children who need my help; how can I use the messages from this research to link the two? And they might add the proviso of taking into account along the way the principles of effective development also described in these pages.

The framework consists of a sequence of five steps. Each step rests on existing approaches or tools in children's services linked in an innovative way. Each step requires sound acknowledgement at least of the evidence in the preceding pages and the research reports from which it has been drawn. The framework provides a mechanism by which change can be experimented with and evaluated prior to being fully implemented. It is not so much a radical solution as a route to that solution.

The value of a clothes peg

Attempting to improve services by applying research messages is a tricky business. Research cannot measure everything. So it picks out factors which act as a good proxy for several others. For example, in their book on secondary schools *15,000 Hours*, Michael Rutter and colleagues counted how many of the schools provided each pupil with their own clothes peg, since this was as good an indicator of a good ethos as any other. The schools with a healthy ethos generally gave each pupil a clothes peg. They did several other things besides, but the clothes peg factor was the one counted. A cynical head of school reading the results might be tempted to introduce clothes pegs—but to no good effect since nothing else connected with a good ethos necessarily follows. Rutter and colleagues' study tells us that schools with a good ethos get better results for its pupils; but gives less attention to how to build a healthy ethos.

What are the needs of children looked after?

For most local authorities, the logical starting point to decision-making about how to change residential services and create other options will be to build up a picture of the needs of 'their' children. In time, as understanding of the available technology improves, it ought to be possible simply to add up each of the individual assessments of children, for example, in the form made possible by the *Looking After Children* records, but for the moment it is necessary to carry out audits–snapshot surveys–of the data already available on the children and to arrive at approximations of the likely demand upon services.

A local authority adopting this approach with respect to residential care will want to know, first, what were the needs of children looked after in the previous year (since they will act as stand-ins for the children coming into care or accommodation in future years). Second, the authority will want to know the needs of children currently in residential settings, since they will require support as services are being developed around them.

There is no single best route to completing this work, but the methods described below make a fairly good starting point. They make it possible to identify different groups of children in need in a local authority and then to design services (including services based on residence) to meet children's needs. It may be that newly-designed services differ markedly and are described very differently from what has been available previously.

WHERE DOES THE EVIDENCE FIT?

Once a clear picture of the needs of children in an authority has been assembled, the evidence described in this overview can be used to help design effective services.

Messages about the continuum first described on page 14 must count for a lot. Where residential care is thought to have a contribution to make, it is essential to consider what other services will operate in combination with it and the timescales for each aspect of the intervention. Clearer answers to questions about expectations for different groups of children will begin to address the concerns set out on page 16.

Evidence about children currently in residential care presented on pages 20-22 will certainly be brought to bear here. Knowledge about who appears to benefit, information on questions of mix, data on those aspects of children's lives that are frequently overlooked–employment needs, their ordinary sexual development–will all help to generate well thought-out solutions to the question of who to place, where, for how long and with what object.

Results from the other parts of the overview are also relevant. A consideration of what should be provided directly by the authority and what should be sought elsewhere will help. An examination of the characteristics of the staff, to include the skills they need to acquire is also desirable. And if the quality of services is to be maintained during the transition, messages about the management of residence discussed on page 33-35 will be valuable, too.

New approaches to children's needs

Local authorities most commonly use the provision available to them and adapt it according to perceived changes in demand. Sometimes their perceptions are based on sound evidence, sometimes not.

Local and health authorities are showing a growing interest in understanding the circumstances of children in need in their locality before designing new services or redesigning existing ones. This is best achieved when built upon systematic record keeping on individual children, such as that provided by the *Looking After Children* system. It can then be built into authority-wide review mechanisms and information management.

The Support Force for Children's Residential Care produced a *Strategic Planning Framework* to help authorities address needs and count resources. It proposes several complementary tools such as *Matching Needs and Services; A Strategic Planning Framework - Part 1: Analysing Need* and *Looking After Children* which can be used to design more effective services.

These approaches have been reasonably successful in identifying future demand for all services for children looked after, including residential care. Generally speaking, they tend to suggest a reduction in the number of children leaving relatives, shorter periods of separation for some, and a higher proportion of those coming into care or accommodation being placed in residential settings. However, the residential services designed as a result of this approach can be quite different from those already in existence.

The approach is particularly helpful with problems of mix. If a local authority is clearer about the needs of children to be looked after in future years, it can be much more precise about who should be placed where.

Being clear about the aims and objectives of residence

Having established the needs of children looked after and how they might be met, a local authority will want to be clear about the objectives of the services it designs to meet those needs, including those that have a residential element.

Objectives are best set at several levels. For example, as Brown and colleagues explain, placements must do what society requires of them. The best guides to such objectives are normally to be found in legislation and guidance, although local interpretation of both may differ. So a formal representation of objectives will be built into each local authority's aims for its services. They will also be clear in the children's services plan and reflected in each residential setting's statement of purpose and function.

All this written material has to be put into practice. So, just as important as these stated objectives, will be a manager's confidence in what can actually be achieved and, as a result of his or her attitude and degree of determination, what staff come to regard as the more practical goals when working with children.

Several studies, principally those that tackled the question of 'what makes a good home?' touch on this issue. The researchers use different words but their conclusions are broadly the same: outcomes tend to be better where objectives are clear, where they can be implemented and where they are in accord with one another and other aspects of children's services, than where they lack clarity, are unattainable or contradictory or undermined by other parts of the personal social services.

Local authorities have a range of mechanisms for establishing objectives. They tend to reflect the characteristics of different organisational structures identified by the Cardiff team. No one route is ideal. The method described on the facing page is only useful insofar as it brings a more logical structure to the task and encourages coordination between different types of planning activity. It will produce for each setting a meaningful statement of purpose and function–something that many seem to have been prepared to do without.

WHERE DOES THE EVIDENCE FIT?

The sections on management, inspection and training (pages 33-38) will be useful because they set the context within which aims are likely to be set. It helps to know who is accountable if an objective is not met, what skills will be required by the staff responsible for delivering the service and that goals will be reviewed to ensure they are met.

Being clear about objectives

Setting objectives can be difficult in complex organisations. The perspective of the Director of Social Services will not necessarily be in tune with the Chief Executive of the Health Authority or Director of Education. In theory, all ought to be at one with the elected members but the reality is often more complicated. The Cardiff study has shown how difficult it can be to navigate the channels of communication that run vertically through large bureaucracies.

The principles of the *Children Act* 1989 set out in the publication *The Care of Children* offer a point of focus for all those involved in setting objectives for children looked after. It sets out 42 principles, including:

- *some that inform good practice*, for example 'admission to public care by virtue of a compulsory order is itself a risk to be balanced against others'
- *some concerned with the quality of services*, for example 'parents should be expected and enabled to retain their responsibilities and to remain as closely involved as is consistent with their child's welfare, even if that child cannot live at home either temporarily or permanently', and
- *some concerned with achieving effective interventions*, for example 'young people should not be disadvantaged or stigmatised by action taken on their behalf, for example as a result of admission to care or to a special residential provision'.

A simple mechanism to encourage greater agreement between objectives for residential centres across children's services and within agency structures is to bring together a small but mixed group of policy makers, managers, clinicians and consumers of services to consider how the principles will be applied in practice.

Given the importance of correspondence between different types of goal, the group should ask:

- what, who, where, when and how questions about applying a principle
- what support will be needed (for example through supervision and training) to ensure tasks are completed
- what review procedures exist to ensure that a principle is applied in practice.

The task just outlined will be made easier if it is undertaken in relation to different groups of children in need emerging from the processes described on page 46. A practice development tool from Dartington called *Structure, Culture and Outcome* tries to make a connection between needs and the cultural life of children's homes.

Ensuring homes are healthy places in which to live

Several research teams came to the central issue of quality control in different ways and from different directions. Most would agree with the general statement that a local authority that knows what it wants from residence and ensures that its homes have clear, commonly recognised objectives is more likely to create healthy living environments for the children it looks after. By the definitions developed in three of the studies, such homes will have strong, positive staff cultures.

Culture can be measured in several ways. The studies by Brown and by Whitaker made use of two complementary perspectives. The former took a series of tasks most likely to occur in a children's home, such as a parent's visit, a child's refusal to go to school or an attack by one resident on another, and asked staff how they would respond. Three patterns of response were identified:

- staff responded differently, signifying a lack of a cultural response
- staff agreed with each other about what they would do, but suggested an unhelpful course of action; a negative culture
- staff agreed on largely helpful responses; a positive culture.

The York study of cultures also deals with staff behaviour in response to circumstances inside and outside children's homes. The researchers used self-esteem as a barometer for a home's well-being: in one where there was high self-esteem at a collective level staff coped well with the steady flow of problems; at the other extreme, groups could be sent into a downward spiral of difficulty by an apparently minor annoyance. In the same vein, the way a local authority interacts with a residential placement can be a strong influence on self-esteem.

Although residential centres with clear objectives tend to be pleasant places in which to live, it is inadvisable to make assumptions about the connection. Monitoring the cultural life inside residential settings and making contingency plans for dealing with even very small problems will demonstrate to residents and carers the links between transparency of aims and quality of care. Asking staff singly and then collectively what they would do in different situations turned out to be a simple but effective mechanism for uncovering potential troublespots.

WHERE DOES THE EVIDENCE FIT?

The section dealing with the homes on pages 23-26 will be of obvious relevance here. The managerial perspective on culture discussed by Whipp and colleagues might also be borne in mind. But more than elsewhere in the process individual studies should be consulted.

Whitaker and colleagues describe a range of difficult situations that regularly occur in children's homes and set out the staff responses–some effective, some not. Farmer and Pollock set out the difficulties posed to foster parents and residential staff by children who have been sexually abused and others who have sexually maltreated other children.

The studies by Dartington concerning the behaviour patterns of extremely difficult young people and the way regime, defined as a coherent method of working with residents, can help or hinder staff.

Arguments about the home culture

Academics will argue long and hard about exactly what is meant by the cultural climate of residence without coming to any agreement. Those who work or live in children's homes usually know exactly what is meant but nevertheless struggle to describe it. Hardly surprising, then, that the methods devised for capturing the essence of a residential culture tend to be flawed.

Brown and colleagues measured culture by the amount of agreement between staff about what to do in ordinary situations.

The tasks were selected from each area of a child's life:

- *where they live*, for example what to do when a new resident arrives
- *their family relations*, for example how to deal with a parent's visit to the home
- *their social and anti-social behaviour*, for example, when one resident hit another
- *their health*, what to do when a resident claims to be too sick to go to school
- *education and employment*, somebody refuses to go to school.

The actual tasks selected may vary.

Farmer and Pollock describe a range of sexual behaviours that require a consistent response.

The York study of young people missing from placements emphasises the problems of running away.

It is important to choose tasks from all aspects of a child's life.

The approach is not so much to pursue the holy grail of a right answer as to find a response that is clearly in the best interests of the child and to which all staff can sign up. Thus, the pursuit is for congruence.

If the findings of the study by Brown and colleagues hold true, authorities that have established clear objectives for their homes will find it easier to establish a healthy culture.

Outcomes for residence and outcomes for children

When they have formulated a strategy those running residential care will want to find out if their expectations for it are realised. For most of the 1990s the word 'outcome' has been used to encompass much of what authorities have needed to know. At the end of the decade the concept of 'best value' is beginning to take its place, implying a rather wider reckoning of good results, reasonable cost and a comparison between similar services.

Whatever the language and conceptual framework, the task of establishing whether residence, in combination with other interventions, is having the desired effect is likely to be on the following lines. First, some way of combining objectives will need to be found, to encompass not only service aims but also the hopes for individual children (or at least groups of children with similar needs). This means embarking on activity that, as part and parcel of the same process, will tell central government what is happening, will inform local and health authority management structures and help home managers to monitor performance and review the progress of residents during and beyond their stay. In the past this work has often been viewed as unconnected activity.

Second, the information that is assembled should illuminate different aspects of services that include residence. There ought to be something about **process** – whether the service is being delivered as expected, then about **outputs** –whether the things the service expects to happen do happen. Most important are **outcomes**, whether or not children's lives are enhanced or at least stabilised by the intervention. Once the data allows comparisons between the different options available for children in need (including doing nothing at all) and some estimation of marginal costs, it ought to be possible to estimate which patterns of intervention yield the best return on the local and health authorities' investment.

WHERE DOES THE EVIDENCE FIT?

The evidence presented in these pages should make it easier to interpret the information on process, output and outcome collected in local authorities. Knowing what proportion of children stay away from school, run away from children's homes, commit crimes, abuse other residents or are maltreated themselves will set useful baselines against which progress can be measured.

There are also messages here for those who may wonder how to respond when the outcomes are less favourable than had been hoped. The passages in the York study of cultures that describe how managers can facilitate steady development of services and how staff cope with homes in danger of taking a 'downward turn' should be useful.

Monitoring Outcomes

Two further monitoring exercises might usefully be applied. First, on a regular basis—and at least annually—the test for a 'good home' used by Sinclair and Gibbs could be applied to all residential centres. Local authorities would review the results so that any correlation between a home's fluctuating fortunes and, for example, leadership, training and recruitment become clear.

Most local authorities use the Department of Health's *Looking After Children* materials (those that have not should consider implementing it especially in relation to children long in residential settings). It will help to identify needs, realistic expectations and outcomes for individual children. As the data accumulate, so will the opportunities for compiling the results from individual children, as well as indicating which homes are achieving good outcomes. It will also provide the evidence on whether the expectations of different combinations of children's services—for example as established in central and local government reviews of public sector services are being met.

A service that includes residence might take the work a step further. The majority of children coming into residence will move on within six months and nearly all will have gone within two years. Contacting all leavers and completing the *Looking After Children* materials a year after departure will provide a valuable 'before' and 'after' picture that could help to adapt practice as well as expressing a continuing commitment to the children.

Repeating the cycle

Barnardo's first institutions were initially seen as a model for the future of children's services. Fifty years later the first strong doubts about the wisdom of residence on such a scale for children in need were being heard; fifty years after that the bulldozers were nosing into the recreation yards.

Today, several hundred pioneers work for scores of agencies that give assistance to several hundred thousand children and their families. Innovations take many forms, but few are properly evaluated and many are abandoned even before they have been rewarded with criticism or review. Understanding what works, for which children in need, when and why has consequently become a priority. The process described in the last few pages can help, and not only with respect to interventions that have a residential component; but to be successful it needs to be applied repeatedly, at least as an annual exercise. Some components, for example, the application of *Looking After Children* should be continuous.

The model proposed here is linear. There is little to be gained from starting in the middle, from using just one part of the approach or from undertaking each stage independently of the others. Modern bureaucracies, it must be said, are not ordinarily designed for step-by-step approaches to problem solving, but that fact remains: efforts for example to bolster staff morale or improve their interpersonal dynamics are unlikely to be of much benefit if the objectives for the team or the needs of the children they are supposed to be helping are left unclear.

A number of methods for completing this work have been described. None is ideal and all have been the subject of criticism of one sort or another, but each is current. They are either being used in a substantial proportion of local authorities or they could be implemented with only the slightest pull on resources. Over time, the selection of methods will change, but the requirement to build up a picture of need that can be used to set complementary objectives for residential care and, in turn, to establish a healthy culture will persist.

If local and health authorities get the measure of this work, they will eventually need to collect much less information, but to do so more often. The goal has to be the sort of refinement of means that will permit data collected for one purpose to be useful for others. Presently, mountains of paperwork are accumulated about many thousands of children in need, yet, as the Bristol team discovered, it is still possible for those looking after children to be unaware of critically important facts.

Finally

This book has suggested a new way of thinking about what is already known about residence. It does not try to promote another new model of an old idea. Observers rightly draw attention to the usefulness of respite care, to the value of the increasingly common foyer models described by Berridge and Brodie or to other adaptations. These have to be encouraged and evaluated, but no single solution will ever be right for all children in need or, for that matter, for all children looked after. The aspiration must be more general: to see what works, for whom, when and why, and continuously to review the findings and adapt the provision.

Management, training, inspection, research and development are other necessary parts of this thinking, but are no more ends in themselves. The research makes it plain that management and training exist to support services established to meet specified objectives. Essentially the scheme recommended here is very simple: there are children in need in society; there are objectives– one hopes achievable ones–for different groups of these children; the appropriate services are designed; management, training, and inspection provide the necessary underpinning.

Getting this scheme in place and doing so in such a way that we can learn as we go would in itself represent a radical change. It would start the process with the child in need and not, as has been the case, with the management structure. It would create training to support professionals charged with meeting needs rather than leaving them to get what they can from what is currently available. And it would lead to inspection that improves our understanding rather than inspection to chastise those who know too little.

If there is clear thinking about the needs of children, and if the same clarity can be brought to deciding the objectives for services and then used to establish a healthier culture for the residential component and to evaluate progress, the result should be better outcomes for children and fewer causes for professional embarrassment.

The evidence suggests that residence should be brought closer into the continuum of services for children in need in order to ensure that the right children come into the sector and find their way to places that are right for them. It also proposes that the quality of life of staff and residents is improved and that the connections between residence and the world outside–with schools, neighbourhoods and families–are strengthened. Much of this should lead to better management, training and inspection. The end result should be more 'good homes' that achieve more for children in need.

The project summaries

Mainly about the children

I	Moving On: Young people and leaving care schemes, 1995	Nina Biehal Jasmine Clayden Mike Stein Jim Wade,	University of York
2	Secure Treatment Outcomes: The care careers of very difficult adolescents, 1998	Roger Bullock Michael Little Spencer Millham,	Dartington Social Research Unit
3	Sexually Abused and Abusing Children in Substitute Care, 1998	Elaine Farmer Sue Pollock,	University of Bristol
4	Going Missing: Young people absent from care (The York study of Going Missing), 1998	Jim Wade Nina Biehal Jasmine Clayden Mike Stein,	University of York

Mainly about the homes

5	Children's Homes Revisited, 1998	David Berridge Isabelle Brodie,	University of Luton
6	Making Residential Care Work: Structure and culture in children's homes, 1998	Elizabeth Brown Roger Bullock Caroline Hobson Michael Little,	Dartington Social Research Unit
7	Private Children's Homes, 1998	Ian Gibbs Ian Sinclair,	University of York
8	A Life without Problems? The achievements of a therapeutic community, 1995	Michael Little Siobhan Kelly,	Dartington Social Research Unit
9	Children's Homes: A study in diversity (The York effectiveness study), 1998	Ian Sinclair Ian Gibbs,	University of York
10	Working in Children's Homes: Challenges and complexities (The York study of cultures), 1998	Dorothy Whitaker Lesley Archer Leslie Hicks,	University of York

Mainly about management & training

11	Evaluating Residential Care Training: Towards qualified leadership, 1998	Dione Hills Camilla Child Julie Hills Vicky Blackburn,	Tavistock Institute
12	The External Management of Children's Homes by Local Authorities, 1999	Richard Whipp Ian Kirkpatrick Martin Kitchener Dianne Owen,	Cardiff University Business School

1 Moving On: Young people and leaving care schemes

Nina Biehal, Jasmine Clayden, Mike Stein, Jim Wade, *University of York*

Specialist leaving care schemes were developed by voluntary agencies and local authority social service departments against a background of research studies highlighting the problems faced by care leavers, amplified by the powerful voices of young people themselves, and the new leaving care responsibilities contained within the *Children Act* 1989. They were intended to provide a focused response to the core needs of care leavers–for accommodation, social support, finance and help with careers.

This research set out to explore three questions. They were, first, to establish what different scheme models existed, what approaches were being developed and what services were they providing; second, to decide how effective such schemes were in helping young people to move on, and, third, to make a comparison between the outcomes and experiences of young people using the schemes and those of leavers who did not use them.

The study was mounted in two stages. Information from social workers was collected in respect of 183 young people who left the care of three local authorities during a six month period. This survey was complemented by a longitudinal and in depth qualitative study of the process of leaving care and of the support offered to 74 leavers by four schemes in the three authorities. The qualitative sample comprised a participating group of young people who received the support of schemes and a comparison group who did not. The young people, their social workers and, where applicable their scheme workers, were interviewed on three occasions during a period of between 18 and 24 months.

The 'follow up' sample of 74 young people, aged between 16 and 19 was made up of 39% men and 61% women. The majority were white (88%); only nine black or mixed heritage young people (12%) took part, but the uneven split reflected the ethnic composition of the leaving care population in the participating authorities. Six (8%) had special support needs. Over half had entered care as teenagers; slightly more left care from foster care (45%) than from residential care (41%). Most had experienced a high degree of movement and disruption during the time they were 'looked after' and were not able to return to their family home. They were thus dependent on social services to equip, prepare and support them in moving on.

The study found that young people continue to leave care at a much earlier age than their peers–a quarter of them when they are only 16. Sometimes it happened because their foster and residential placements broke down, but often, particularly in children's homes, it was merely assumed that they should move on when they reached the age of 16 or 17. As for where they went, just under a half of the group moved to transitional accommodation such as hostels, lodgings and stays with friends. A small group, approximately 20%, moved immediately to independent accommodation but the figure had risen to well over half two years later.

The leaving care schemes all played a major part in the 'moving on' process, by preparing young people, by providing ongoing support and in meeting their accommodation needs. Between them, the schemes were able

The study looks at young people leaving care and accommodation and examines the extent to which different types of leaving care schemes aid this transition, whether in terms of practical help, such as accommodation and employment, or personal supports, such as boosting self-esteem and social competence.

The approach of life course analysis aims to tease out the ways in which the young people's transitions are structured both by their personal histories and relationships and by the broader social and economic context in which their lives unfold.

to offer directly managed accommodation in trainer flats or specialist hostels, 'floating support' schemes, access to supported lodgings or hostels and support for young people in their own tenancies. Even for those young people experiencing the greatest instability, continuity of support often prevented a descent into homelessness or else provided a rapid escape from it. The schemes were able to help the great majority of care leavers to find and maintain good accommodation within two years.

Consistent with previous findings, it emerged that educational and employment outcomes were generally poor compared to those for young people in the population at large. For the majority, care was unable to compensate them for their damaging pre-care experiences and thus did not establish a successful pattern of schooling or a career path. As a result half were unemployed within a few months of leaving care and nearly two thirds failed to establish any stable employment pattern. They faced periods of short-term casual work interspersed with episodes of training and unemployment. Another consequence was that most were living on or near benefit levels. Poor educational attainment and its knock-on effect on career prospects were associated with a high degree of movement while being looked after.

All the schemes had a central role in arranging and administering financial assistance. However the developmental role of promoting education, training and employment was less advanced than other aspects.

Leaving care was associated with a moment when many young people were trying to make sense of their pasts, to trace missing parents or generally to find continuity in their lives and a sense of belonging. The study found that maintaining family links and having an opportunity to explore personal histories were associated with a positive identity and thus with the ability to build a more secure platform for the future. Even where family relationships were poor, family links, including those with brothers and sisters, grandparents and other members of the extended family, were very important to most. Among black and mixed heritage young people the sense of ethnic identity tended to change over time; their identification with a particular group was strongly related to their oneness with or rejection of family members.

The schemes often played only a minimal role in mediating between young people and their families, because of an assumption, often an erroneous one, that field social workers were still taking responsibility for considerations of that kind. On the other hand, they were very active in helping young people to develop their friendship networks by drawing on specialist knowledge of the local youth and leisure services provision as well as running their own groups and 'drop in' activities. This was felt to be a useful contribution since, in terms of outcomes, those with a secure sense of identity had good or fair social networks, positive family relationships and good relationship skills.

The research set out to assess different leaving care schemes but it was difficult to establish any blueprint for an ideal hybrid as a result. The four schemes differed in their perspective, methods of working and in the balance sought between 'young person demand led' and 'planned worker

While the *Children Act* 1989 has helped to raise the profile of leaving care and stimulate the development of services, the balance between the duties and powers within it has meant that regional and local variations persist in the level of services available to young people.

Few residential staff were able to offer continuing support once young people had moved on and homes were not always welcoming to returners. In residential placements, there was often an assumption that young people should move on once they reach the age of 16 and 17. Children's homes also need to adopt strategies to promote a positive culture of educational achievement: only three leavers from residential backgrounds attained any qualifications.

led' services. Each scheme adopted a different approach and each had different strengths.

The specialist schemes were found to make a positive contribution to specific outcomes in respect of accommodation, life skills and furthering social networks. It was also evident that they worked well at a general level with three quarters of young people either in achieving positive outcomes or in making progress towards such outcomes in terms of accommodation, a regular source of income and a sense of self esteem (particularly bearing in mind the highly disadvantaged starting points). But they can only build on what has gone before: stability, continuity, sound family links, uninterrupted education, good preparation and a flexible approach to leaving are the foundation stones.

2 Secure Treatment Outcomes: The care careers of very difficult adolescents

Roger Bullock, Michael Little, Spencer Millham, *Dartington Social Research Unit*

Only a minority of young people in residential care are placed in secure accommodation, yet its use generates considerable concern. It raises moral unease associated with locking up children and provokes questions about the value for money. The Dartington Unit has charted the care careers of a particular group of young people in security, namely very difficult and disturbed adolescents admitted to long stay secure treatment units of whom there are about 150 in England and Wales at any one time. The study followed the progress of 204 of them for two years after leaving. It explored their characteristics, treatment experiences and subsequent careers.

As would be expected, young people classified as very difficult and disturbed display severe and sometimes chronic problems. As a group, they have a higher than average rate for almost every social disadvantage and behavioural difficulty. Often they will have exhausted the best facilities of social services, health and education and, because of the dangers they pose to themselves or to others, become suitable candidates for security.

The research identified the legal and administrative avenues along which young people move. It shows the complexity of the decision making process which rests on a mixture of clear legal criteria and professional judgements, all made within the context of a service that is largely provision-led. It also shows that young people's background factors and responses to interventions interact with decisions made by professionals and/or the courts to produce a distinctive career route at the end of which lies entry to a secure unit.

The study identified five such career routes: being in long-term state care; being in long-term special education until mid-adolescence before becoming the responsibility of social services; having no previous welfare involvement until difficult behaviour 'erupts' and rapidly deteriorates; being a one-off grave offender; and, being a serious and persistent offender.

This study follows the progress of young people from the point of entry to long-stay secure treatment units until two years after leaving. Outcomes in six areas of their lives are charted and linked to presenting problems, the type of intervention offered and any protective factors in the young person's background.

A feature of young people who become candidates for long-term security is their tendency to present problems which cannot be met effectively by a single agency or intervention. Frequently, the result is an eclectic approach that attempts to incorporate the best features of several specialisms.

At the point of admission, the best and worst scenarios for each career routes were predicted from research knowledge about what happens to difficult adolescents and the predictions were tested against subsequent events. By these means, it was possible to estimate the contribution to their progress of the young people's personal resources and of the treatment intervention they received. The researchers were also able to take account of influences (protective factors) which appeared to modify risks once young people left the units.

It was found that outcomes were reasonably predictable using the research knowledge available. Thus, better care and control and carefully targeted services earlier on might have obviated much subsequent turmoil, upset, time and expense. Moreover, young people could sometimes make considerable progress while in the units. For example, on admission, nine out of 10 had criminal convictions and 70% had been found guilty of a serious offence. But while they were in security, their misbehaviour diminished, and, after leaving, re-offending was less common than might have been anticipated. Indeed, the levels of serious crime were much reduced.

When a comparison was made with 'look alikes' placed elsewhere, it was found that the specialist treatment centres did better with very difficult cases than secure units run by local authorities or young offender institutions run by the Prison Department. The centres were also more successful with some groups of young people than others. For example, those who stayed full time in a centre which attempted psycho-therapeutic treatment and who were on a career route other than long term state care were six times more likely to be well adjusted socially two years after leaving than had other conditions applied.

This information was supplemented by further analysis in which information about outcomes from a retrospective study of leavers was used to forecast what would happen to individuals for whom the outcome was unknown. The prediction was then modified in light of any known protective factors. This showed that, even for those who entered the units with massive deficits, treatment could make a difference. The outcomes reflected the time and effort taken by the institution concerned and the sophistication of the approach. Where need was identified by the treatment centres and where interventions addressed that need, better outcomes were achieved (within the range expected for each career group). Where a protective factor, for example arising from an enabling personality characteristic or helpful family situation, came into play, outcomes were better still. Where neither protective factors nor interventions helped nor changed the young person, the worst predictions were likely to be more accurate.

Outcomes based on reconviction within two years of leaving were found to be best from the specialist treatment centres, next best from the medium intensive local authority settings and worst from prison department custody. Whilst there was no certainty of 'cure' in the treatment offered, even in the most sophisticated secure centres, those who received no treatment generally fared worse.

Young people's care careers were found to reflect an interaction between all the factors described: the combination of background characteristics, care

Two dimensions of troubled children's lives were used to understand what happened to the young people. The first was 'life route', that is to say the decisions that a young person (and his or her family) made which affected life chances. The second was 'process', defined as the decisions made by professionals and/or courts (in response to the young person's life route) which affected life chances. The interaction between these two dimensions was subsumed under the general term 'career route'.

Inevitably with such a group of young people, there were some shocking stories to report. But there were also some successes that were just as remarkable. For the great majority, the outcome was somewhere between these extremes.

The most disappointing results were to do with outputs; that is to say with judgements of professional activity. The contrast between what the young people received inside specialist treatment centres and outside after they left was frequently sharp. Local authorities were capable of investing several hundred thousand pounds in an individual who stayed in state care up to the age of 18 years, but they often did very little thereafter.

careers and the interventions applied. Within broad parameters, the career route prior to moving into a specialist centre can be used to predict where and with whom the young people will live, how well they will get on with families, what sort of jobs they will get and so on. The combination of the nature, quality and relevance to their needs of treatment interventions was shown to make the difference between young people reaching their potential or drifting into circumstances that made a much worse outcome more likely.

3 Sexually Abused and Abusing Children in Substitute Care

Elaine Farmer, Sue Pollock, *University of Bristol*

In spite of high levels of concern among professionals about how best to manage sexually abused children and young abusers who are looked after there has been little research. This study aimed to fill some of the gaps by examining how such children were managed in residential and foster care, the interventions and treatment provided for them, the mix of children within different settings and the steps taken to keep them safe from other residents and from adults.

The fieldwork was conducted in two local authorities. The first phase was a review of the case files in the two local authorities of all 250 children who had been newly looked after during a set period. A comparison was made between the characteristics and care histories of the sexually abused/abusing children and those of the non-victimised/victimising. In the second phase of the work, a sub-sample of 40 sexually abused/abusing young people aged 10 or over was drawn. Interviews were conducted with key residential workers or foster carers, social workers and with the young people themselves. In addition, a range of standardised measures relating to the young people's behaviour and well-being was applied.

Almost two in five (38%) of all the children who entered substitute care in the two local authorities had been sexually abused or had abused another child. The sexually abused/abusing children were found to be more disadvantaged than the other looked after children in that they were significantly more likely to have had their names placed at some time on the child protection register (under any category), to have had a previous care experience and to have spent longer in care. In addition, tests of statistical significance showed that the sexually abused/abusing children were more likely to have had severe educational problems (non-attendance and school exclusion, serious behaviour problems at school, being bullied), to have experienced rejection and disrupted parenting (that is multiple separations from their main parent, a parent who had multiple partners, and care which adversely affected their emotional development) and to have been seen as troublesome (that is serious behaviour problems and being beyond control at home). In addition, the girls were more likely to have become pregnant.

This study considers how sexually abused children and young abusers are managed while they are living in substitute care. Particular attention is paid to the interventions provided and to the consequences of mixing young people who have a history of sexual abuse or of abusing with others.

It emerged from the follow-up sample that information about sexual abuse in the case histories of 42% of the abused children had not been passed on to the care givers at the time of placement and that in over half the cases where children had sexually abused others, the information was not shared with the residential or foster carers. Two fifths of carers complained that they were given insufficient information at the point of placement.

Once looked after, a number of other differences emerged. More of the sexually abused/abusing children had more moves in care in the first six months after admission and significantly more of the abused and abusing children showed new behaviour problems.

When children with a background of sexual abuse or sexually abusing behaviour were scrutinised, it was found that fewer than one in five entered care for this reason, so this aspect of their history was easily overlooked. Moreover, incidents of abuse or abusing behaviour were poorly recorded, partly because many had not been dealt with under the aegis of child protection procedures. Since key information about children's histories was not held centrally on case files, new social workers sometimes did not know about past abuse or else the facts were minimised in order to secure placements.

During their placement in residential or foster care, the young people both faced and presented a number of risks. A third of the interview sample (12 girls and a boy) were sexually abused, had frequently been involved in prostitution or were vulnerable to sexual exploitation. Almost one in five of the girls (4 of the 22) became pregnant and over one in five of the girls (5 of the 22) alleged that they had been raped or sexually assaulted during the placement. Of the latter, there were two allegations of sexual assault by a resident or staff member in residential care and three instances of rape or sexual assault on young people while they were outside the care setting.

During the placement which constituted the focus of the study (the index placement) almost one in five (7 of 36) of the victimised young people sexually abused another child and a similar proportion of children (3 of 17) who had already sexually abused a child repeated this behaviour. This was mainly abuse of other residents in children's homes, the children and grandchildren of foster carers, other fostered children and siblings. Overall, two thirds of the young people in the interview sample (27/40) became involved in sexual activities or showed sexual behaviours which put themselves or others at risk. In spite of these risks there was a tendency for caregivers and social workers to normalise these sexual behaviours and to develop high thresholds before action was taken. This was particularly true for sexual behaviour that occurred *outside* the care setting, such as indiscriminate sexual activity and prostitution.

During the index placement fewer than a third of the abused young people were provided with work on the abuse itself, either from specialist counsellors or social workers. It was worrying that only one of the young people in the interview sample received therapeutic help which addressed the abusing behaviour. Even when help was offered, caregivers were rarely informed about what occurred in the sessions, although they were sometimes left to pick up the pieces when a child returned to a placement in an aggressive or unpredictable frame of mind. This was unfortunate because it weakened the ability of young people to integrate the gains from the therapeutic work into their everyday lives. Forty five per cent of the young people talked to their caregivers or social workers either fully or partially about the abuse or the events connected to it. Only one talked about her abusing behaviour and even then not in depth.

Half the sexually abused young people in the study abused another child at some stage, generally another child in care. This evidence suggested a likely connection in some cases between the experience of sexual abuse and the later development of sexually abusing behaviour.

Sexual abuse was part of a pattern of disadvantage which had serious emotional consequences for the majority of the young people. Among those in the interview sample, nearly 70% had suffered previous physical abuse, over a third had been severely neglected, 30% had undergone multiple separations from parents, 50% had experienced severe rejection or scapegoating, more than 50% had witnessed violence between their parents, 80% were considered to have been beyond control at home and nearly 60% had harmed themselves or attempted suicide.

It became clear that good practice required caregivers to make it clear to children both that they knew about their past difficulties and that the children were free to talk about it at any time. While this acknowledgement would not necessarily lead to an open discussion, it would at least leave the way open. It was important, however, not to underestimate how difficult such openness could be for caregivers who varied widely in their willingness and capacity to attend to young people's accounts and often felt unprepared and unsupported.

The best outcomes in terms of behavioural gains were for those who were encouraged to explore their difficult experiences and feelings both in a therapeutic relationship and in their everyday lives in care. However, over half had never received any therapeutic help that addressed their sexual abuse. Three distinct sub-groups stood out as raising particular management and placement issues.

YOUNG ABUSERS

Most were boys of whom a high proportion (41%) had learning difficulties and the great majority emotional and behavioural problems. They often came from highly sexualised backgrounds. The majority were placed in foster care with experienced carers and most of the remainder entered specialist residential placements, including secure provision. The management of abusers while in placement generally consisted of tight supervision but, with one exception, there was no work which focused on the abusing behaviour itself.

Experienced caregivers tended to be well engaged and to provide good care. Short-term outcomes were fairly good, in that behaviour improved and major needs were adequately met. However, because of the lack of therapeutic intervention there was a danger that their abusing behaviour would resurface after leaving care.

SEXUALISED ADOLESCENT GIRLS

Almost two thirds of the children who were known only to have been sexually abused had emotional and behavioural problems. As many as 71% rated themselves on the child depression inventory as having suicidal thoughts and self-harm was not uncommon. The majority of the abused young children were girls most of whom were placed in ordinary children's homes.

Girls who made indiscriminate sexual approaches to the boys and men they met raised the anxieties of residential and foster carers. They were uncertain about how to manage such behaviour and male caregivers distanced themselves for fear of allegations being made against them.

Inside the placements, although many examples of good practice were found, most caregivers lacked ideas about how to deal with teenage girls who sexualised physical contact but whose backgrounds indicated a clear need for affection. They were generally at a loss, too, as to how to deal with girls who were sexually indiscriminate or were involved in sexually exploitative relationships *outside* their placements, although two children's homes and some foster carers had found effective ways to exercise such supervision.

Because of the uncertainty about how to manage their behaviour the wider needs of these girls were not well met. Their school attendance was very poor and many had few, if any, leisure activities. Outcomes for girls exhibiting sexualised behaviour were among the poorest of all the children in the study and they continued to be at risk.

CHILDREN INVOLVED IN PROSTITUTION

The only group with worse outcomes were children involved in prostitution. One in five of the young people in the study had been involved in or were on

For victims of sexual abuse and for abusers, the best outcomes occurred when young people had been helped to explore their difficult experiences and feelings with a counsellor and within the placement. The need for special support from outside residence is emphasised by the finding that two in three of the sexually abused adolescents had or were on the borderline of a clinical disorder. However, there was little evidence in care planning that information from assessments was used to evaluate the need for therapeutic intervention.

Young perpetrators in whose behaviour sex and aggression were linked required specialist placements that provided tight supervision with access to therapeutic help.

There were a number of areas in which children could have been better served while they were being looked after. More attention could have been paid to educational needs, especially in view of the fact that almost half had histories of non-school attendance and a third had been excluded from school at some time. More priority needed to be given to providing information about sexual relationships and contraceptive advice: the children in the sample were very poorly informed at the same time as being highly sexually active and so the the risk of pregnancy and of sexually transmitted disease was high.

the fringes of prostitution during their placements, while absconding or after discharge from care. Three procured other residents for the purpose. Young people who became involved were extremely difficult to contain, partly because they persistently absconded, partly because care-givers had little success in altering their behaviour.

There was a real scarcity of ideas about how to engage and contain them apart from the use of secure units. All the same, it was clear that a rapid response was needed in order to try to influence the child's choice of associates before the behaviour became entrenched and before other children had been drawn in. Remoteness from the child's networks appeared to be one important ingredient of a good placement.

Overall, about half the foster carers and residential workers reported experiencing considerable stress. Given the extent of the young people's disturbance and the trauma in their lives there was a clear need for better training, increased levels of support and regular consultancy .

4 Going Missing: Young people absent from care
Jim Wade, Nina Biehal, Jasmine Clayden, Mike Stein, *University of York*

Renewed concern in the 1980s about the plight of young runaways, primarily from the family home, led to a number of studies concerned with mapping numbers, identifying motivations and charting careers. With regard to those in substitute care, the studies showed that running away was primarily a problem of the mid teen years, that around 30% of all runaways were going missing from residential care, that they tended to do so more often and for longer periods, and that many of those who went missing from residential care had first run away from the family home. The findings suggested, therefore, that going missing needed to be understood, at least in part, in relation to young people's early experiences in the family home and, perhaps, as an effect of the interplay between past experience and current placement contexts.

Against this background the researchers set out to investigate going missing from substitute care, including residential and foster placements. There were two phases to the study. The first, to which the findings discussed here relate, involved an investigation of patterns of going missing by means of two surveys in four local authorities covering a twelve month period. The second phase was based on interviews with young people, social workers and carers and explored the contexts, histories, motivations and experiences of young people going missing and the range of professional responses to them. Information was collected on a range of unauthorised absences, including those which might be defined as running away, by asking social workers and residential social workers/foster carers to complete a questionnaire when a young person had either been missing overnight or reported to the police as missing.

In the main survey, information was collected on 210 young people and included data on a single incident of unauthorised absence together with information on family backgrounds, care careers, history of going missing and other issues. A second supplementary survey of all in-house children's

This study explores the nature and extent of running away from state care. Particular attention is paid to the interventions provided and to the consequences of mixing young people who have a history of sexual abuse or of abusing others.

homes in the four authorities was also undertaken. Questionnaires were returned by 32 children's homes covering all incidents of unauthorised absence during the same 12 month period as the main survey.

From this latter survey it emerged that 43% of all 11-16 year olds accommodated in residential units managed by the four authorities went missing at least once during the twelve month period; 272 young people accounting for 2,227 incidents. Variations between the authorities were marked, ranging from 25% to 71% of all those accommodated. Variations between units were also observed. Of the 32 homes surveyed, just four homes accommodated 42% of those who went missing.

Accurate figures for foster placements were impossible to obtain, due to inadequacies in the authorities' recording procedures, but from the main survey it was estimated that at least 5% of 11-16 year olds accommodated in foster placements went missing at least once during the year, a probable under-estimate.

None of the authorities had a clear idea of the scale of the problem nor where pockets of high absence might exist. Although children's homes were required to keep an accurate daily log, which included unauthorised absences, they were not centrally collated. No data was routinely collected for absences from foster placements unless social workers happened to record them in casework files. Files were often inaccurate, especially for those young people who went missing often. Proper record keeping and the central collation of data represent essential prerequisites for monitoring absences, identifying pockets of high absence and planning strategic interventions.

The findings confirmed that going missing was primarily a problem of the mid and late teen years. Half were aged 14 or 15 and the average age for first going missing was 13. Gender and ethnic origin were not closely associated with differences in the pattern of young people's histories of going missing nor in the contours of the particular absence. However, young people with emotional and behavioural difficulties first went missing at a younger age, tended to go missing more often, were twice as likely to be excluded from school and were more likely to have committed a criminal offence. Patterns of going missing and the risks of detachment were therefore more extreme for this group.

Perhaps not surprisingly, a greater proportion of young people in the residential sector had a more protracted history of going missing. They tended to have gone missing first at an earlier age, had done so more often in total and were more likely to have had a past conviction for offending than was the case for those in foster homes.

Information was collected about one specific absence. Just over half the sample were considered to have gone missing to be with 'friends or family' (friends group), the vast majority with friends, and just under half had 'run away or stayed out' (runaways group). Patterns associated with the absence were distinctive. The 'friends group' comprised more older teenagers, more often from fostering backgrounds. Their absences tended to be less problem focused, less associated with offending and, while they tended to stay away longer, they were more likely to return voluntarily. In contrast, the 'runaways

Despite attempts to identify distinguishing factors, previous research had found no difference between children who ran away and those who did not (other than the level of their offending). Absconding could not be explained in terms of individual characteristics - there was no such thing as a runaway type. Psychologists concluded that absconding was 'learned behaviour' and that positive or negative reinforcement contributed to whether it continued or ceased. This was an important finding because it shifted the focus much more towards processes and context and away from individual characteristics.

group' tended to be younger, more often from residential placements and their absence was more likely to have had a problem focus (more often placement centred). They were more likely to have slept rough, to have offended while away and were less likely to have returned voluntarily. By most yardsticks these young people appeared at greater risk. Differences in approach are suggested in the study: a more flexible negotiated approach that helps to lessen the need to go missing may be more appropriate for those fitting the profile of the 'friends group', while the 'runaways' profile brings the need for protection and firm boundaries into sharper focus.

Looking at the absence more generally, the majority went alone (55%), did not travel far, returned voluntarily (52%) and did not stay away any longer than was the case in previous study samples. However, over a quarter (28%) were known to have been at risk while away (including offending, substance misuse and being the victim of crime)–a likely under-estimate given that a half of social workers/carers did not know one way or the other. Over a quarter (28%) were also unaware where their young person had stayed while away. Where there was information, three quarters had stayed with friends or family, the majority with friends, and 15% slept rough. Over one third of those who ran away slept rough and two thirds of those sleeping rough were aged 11-13 and clearly at considerable risk.

School non-attendance, exclusion and a criminal conviction at the time of going missing were higher for this sample than is the case for the looked after population generally. However, whilst non-attendance and offending are both associated with going missing often, the link with offending is the stronger one.

Going missing often was associated with a growing risk of detachment from the centres of adult authority for teenagers. Those missing more often were more likely to have experienced high levels of placement movement, to be experiencing problems in their current placement, to be not attending or excluded from school and to have involvement in offending and substance misuse. Whilst true for all, these associations were more true for some than for others. The risk of detachment was greater for those who fitted the profile of the 'runaways group'. These connections pointed to the need for early intervention on an inter-agency basis. Once the pattern became set the possibilities for engaging the young person and resolving underlying difficulties were likely to become more remote.

Just under half the sample (46%) first went missing from the family home and there was evidence that these groups (the family and care groups) formed distinctive sub-groupings within the sample. The 'family group' was twice as likely to contain teenage entrants who were older at the time of the survey and were more likely to be disaffected. Despite having been looked after a shorter time and experiencing less placement movement, overall they had gone missing more often, were less likely to be attending school and more likely to have committed offences and been involved in substance misuse. For this group, patterns of going missing and detachment were rooted in the family home and were already taking shape prior to being looked after. Their subsequent care careers appeared to have less impact upon these patterns. In contrast, the 'care group' tended to be younger, had been looked after longer, showed more signs of attachment to school and less involvement in offending and substance misuse. However, for those in this group who had gone missing often, instability in their care careers (as measured by placement movement) was more closely associated with their tendency to go missing.

Patterns associated with the 'home group' pointed to the need for greater emphasis to be placed on preventive work with teenagers whilst in the family home and, once looked after, for intensive support to help break the emergence of a persistent pattern. For the 'care group', given the association between instability and going missing often, efforts directed at maintaining the structure of a stable placement, regular school attendance and diversion from offending were thought likely to prove protective.

5 Children's Homes Revisited

David Berridge, Isabelle Brodie, *University of Luton*

This research undertakes the difficult and unusual task of analysing change in residential child care over a decade. It does so, firstly, by looking at policy and attitude changes in the general social services context and, secondly, by examining what has happened in the past decade with regard to the structure and use of residential care in the three local authorities which participated in the earlier research discussed in *Children's Homes* (Berridge, 1985).

The general findings about local authority policies indicate considerable changes over the past ten years in the number of young people being accommodated and in the number and size of homes. They also point to the considerable and often neglected group of children and young people with learning, physical and sensory impairments accommodated under respite care arrangements ('short breaks'). These changes in policy and legislation are explored in the context of wider social and economic factors. The authors also draw together substantive child care research which has demonstrated that, for comparable groups of young people, children's homes are equally effective as foster care in meeting their objectives.

For the detailed study of residential homes 12 were selected which reflected current patterns of use and were, therefore, comparable with those studied in 1985. The report describes who lives in them and why, the characteristics of the workforce, how establishments are organised and run, the links with networks around homes and the quality of care now being offered. It takes into account the perspectives of the children and young people, of the managers–and of the researchers who based their responses on participant observation. Biographical information on young people and staff was also gathered.

The pattern of participant observation in the homes was determined by a schedule which ranged from comment on the physical appearance of the homes to an examination of the daily routine inside them. The nature of

In this research, the results of a study of children's homes undertaken in the early 1980s are compared with those of a similar survey conducted ten years later. The characteristics of the children and staff and the quality of care are reassessed. The implications of these trends for the future of residential child care are discussed.

Comparisons between old and new populations showed increasing age differentiation, more girls, fewer sibling groups, more children with histories of abuse and behaviour problems and shorter stays. No staff lived in the homes any more. There were some welcome changes, such as greater contact between children and families and between staff and families, but other aspects, such as the availability of specialist resources and the quality of inter-agency work, continued to be unsatisfactory.

interaction between young people and staff and their activities was described and contrasted with the situation found in the 1985 research.

Comparing the current situation with that in 1985, the study found that only four of the original homes still existed, that no staff now lived on site and that only four of the 136 interviewed in the first study still worked for the same employer. The numbers of residential places in the three local authorities had dwindled by three-quarters.

Four categories of homes are identified and compared: local authority homes for adolescents; local authority homes for younger children; local authority homes offering short breaks for young people with severe learning disabilities and additional health needs; and private children's homes. Greater age differentiation was found in the local authority homes than the private ones. Compared with the homes for adolescents, the other categories were more successful in achieving attendance at school. Private homes mostly had their own schools on the premises.

Few of the homes in the new study had Statements of Purpose and those that had been written were often general and out of date. Most homes had not developed any strategy to meet the needs of girls, ethnic minorities or care leavers. Whilst relationships between staff and young people were informal and friendly, behavioural control of adolescents was a major issue, although staff working with young people with disabilities were noticeably less anxious about behaviour management.

A third of the residents were under 12 and most had multiple problems leading to their being looked after. Aside from the children with disabilities, most residents were known to have experienced abuse prior to their entry to accommodation—an increase compared to the situation in 1985. The incidence of behavioural problems had doubled; the average length of stay had more than halved.

Staff in the current study were greater in number, slightly better qualified and had more experience than their predecessors. There were more male staff than ten years previously and more job changes were reported. As in other research summarised here, staff felt that the young people they cared for had become more difficult to manage. The level of support from external management had declined since 1985 and was felt by staff to be insufficient for their needs. The status of residential workers remained low.

Staff in all categories of home often lacked essential information about the children, such as their ethnic origin, religion, child protection registration status and whether or not a statement of special educational needs existed. Staff were positive about maintaining contacts with birth families, even though parental visits to the homes were infrequent. Relationships with parents had noticeably improved over the years. Disconcertingly, relationships with field workers were said to be worse than those with external professionals, such as the police. There were also signs of strain in relations with neighbours: most were hostile to the presence of a home.

Inter-agency and multi-professional aspects of the work were felt to have deteriorated since 1985 and the resources for such activity were limited. For example, there was virtually no specialist input to help staff plan working methods and regimes or to respond to educational problems. Indeed, there

The authors describe an enhanced, integrated model of residential care based on the positive aspects of provision for young people with severe learning difficulties and additional health needs. The distinguishing features of the approach are to be found in the areas of relationships with children's families, public/social attitudes to the work, inter-professional working and practice style.

was a noticeable absence of high quality learning materials even though school non-attendance was a major problem in the adolescent homes. Few therapeutic resources were available, except to children with disabilities, and there was a dearth of professional help generally for young people with behavioural, educational, offending, personal and psychiatric problems.

Residential care for children and young people with disabilities was found to be perceived and resourced quite differently from other categories of home. Short breaks were used as a service to parents and children and were part of long-term planning and family support. Staff working in this field felt they had higher status than residential staff elsewhere, a reflection perhaps of the fact that affluent and articulate parents used and valued the service they provided. The model of care emphasised the benefits of adopting broad development objectives and the need for young people to gain instrumental skills. Behaviour management was not a preoccupation. However, there was some ambivalence about the merits of parental contact and residents were generally consulted less. The relatively large numbers of staff in such homes could be a source of discontinuity and confusion.

Standards of residential practice were found to be highly uneven across the four categories of homes. Planned, coherent professional procedures were uncommon. In judging the quality of homes, three of the 12 were rated as 'good', eight as 'average' and one as 'poor'. It appeared to the researchers that compared with the 1985 sample, there were fewer homes in the 'good' and 'poor' categories and more that were 'average'. The 'best' homes spread across categories and more variation was found within each category than between them. The extent of young people's problems did not determine the quality of care that could be offered.

Staff morale correlated highly with quality of care. As with Sinclair and Gibbs's study, it was found that structural factors, such as staffing ratios and qualifications, were unrelated to the quality of service. There was a strong association between the quality of care and the extent to which unit managers could state objectives for a home and keep to them, and with procedures that permitted some control over admissions. A manager's ability to express a clear theoretical or therapeutic orientation or clear working methods and stability among the staff group were also beneficial for the quality of care.

Overall, homes scored high for the quality of staff/child relationships but lower for the educational environment within homes. The four homes that scored highest came from different categories. And there was more variation within categories of home than between them.

6 Making Residential Care Work: Structure and culture in children's homes
Elizabeth Brown, Roger Bullock, Caroline Hobson, Michael Little, *Dartington Social Research Unit*

Research into the dynamics of residential care flourished in the 1960s. Interest in regimes and their effects on staff and residents produced several publications (eg Goffman, Polsky) which still influence thinking. However, the context of residential care in Britain has changed radically since then and it may be that the perspective adopted by these earlier researchers is no longer useful. Indeed, the findings may no longer apply as homes are much

This study explores the relationship between the structure of a home and the staff and child cultures that develop in it and the consequences for the success of the home and the care careers of the children.

smaller, children's stays are shorter, there are many more staff, regimes are less institutional and residential care is likely to be only part of the services provided to children and families.

The first aim of this investigation was to reconsider the concepts of structure and culture and to assess their value for understanding children's homes. One of the problems of the earlier research was that it was difficult to separate cause and effect. It tended to produce a circular argument which ran as follows: a good home is one where staff understand and believe in their work; staff are like this because they work in a good home. The second aim was, therefore, to try and identify a causal rather than a descriptive process. This would help explain what led to what and how change could be effected.

Thirdly, the exercise would be somewhat limited if its findings had little application, so there was a need to assess whether any causal relationships between structure and culture found in the study had an effect: on (i) outcomes for the home, and (ii) the welfare of children and families. It was hoped that the overall result would be to identify the essential features of a 'good' home and to clarify the benefits to the children.

The study was undertaken in nine community homes chosen to be representative of those in England and Wales in terms of their size, function, location and administrative category. At the start of the research, they cared for 65 children in establishments varying in size between five and 11 beds. Three could look after children for long periods, and four admitted children in emergencies. The number of child care staff in each home ranged from eight to 22. Six were run by local authorities, two by voluntary organisations and one was a private business.

The terms 'structure' and 'culture' evolved from long-standing interest at Dartington and elsewhere in the formal and informal worlds of residence. The structure of the homes was analysed by considering three types of objective: societal goals, defined as those implied by law or expectations in society; the formal goals, which are local adaptations of societal goals by managers and their implementation in practice; and belief goals which reflect the underlying values of managers and staff. The extent of 'concordance' between the three sets of goals was a key variable across the homes. In some homes the goals were far more complementary and mutually reinforcing than in others.

The analysis of staff and child cultures was undertaken by considering responses to common situations that arise in residential care, such as a child's arrival, a birthday or a tantrum. Where there was a clear group response, cultures were deemed to be strong in that particular area. Where the response complemented the aims of the home, it was considered to be positive.

The separate concern with outcome rested on external measures used to assess each home's performance and the progress of the children they looked after. Twelve measures were used to indicate performance, including how staff, children and other visitors saw the home; how staff and children were observed to behave in the home, and the quality of practice relative to the standards specified by the *Children Act* 1989. Outcomes for children

The terms 'structure' and 'culture' are hardly new and some observers might argue that the plethora of institutional research in the 1960s left little new to say. But, the context of children's homes today is very different. It is unlikely that the adult regimes described by Goffman and Sykes, with their violent and exploitative undercultures, can be considered to reflect life in community homes looking after children in need in the 1990s.

were judged in three ways. First, a set of criteria indicated in legislation and guidance as good child care practice was applied. Second, for two children in each home, two assessments of progress were made, using the *Looking After Children* materials to map changes in their situation and to identify outcomes. Third, actual outcomes were compared with predictions of the best and worst scenarios made by the researchers and based on research knowledge at the point of admission.

Homes were studied over a period of 12 months. A wide range of data was collected: it included information on the home itself and on the backgrounds of staff and children; material in files, reports and official documents; interview replies from staff and children; data from standardised tests and questionnaires; evidence from non-participant observation; and follow-up studies which paid close attention to the experiences over one year of the two staff and two children in each home.

The evidence supported a linear causal model in which structure determined staff culture, which in turn determined child culture. A children's home with concordant societal, formal and belief goals produced a strong staff culture which supported the aims of the home, and either a strong child culture which also supported the formal goals or a fragmented child culture which did not undermine it. Such homes were of high quality in that they were able to demonstrate good outcomes both for the homes themselves and the children who lived there.

In three homes there was concordance between the formal goals (the expressed aims of the staff and managers) which were broadly in tune with the principles of the *Children Act* (the societal goals). In three other homes, there was ambiguity and in two others, there was a level of discord, sufficient to cause serious problems. In the remaining home the pattern was unclear.

Four patterns of relationship between structure and culture were found among the nine homes studied:
- a high level of concordance between societal, formal and belief goals, which created a healthy staff culture supportive of the aims and objectives of the home, and in which the child culture complemented the aims of the home (three homes fell into this category)
- some discord in the structure which produced problematic staff and child cultures, which were mixed in terms of their strength and orientation, so limiting but not greatly damaging the achievements of the homes (three homes fell into this category)
- highly discordant structures that generated strong and counterproductive staff cultures, as a result of which staff strove to get through the day unscathed (two homes fell into this category)
- an unclear relationship where there was average concordance in the structure but weak and generally negative staff and child cultures (one home fell into this category).

It is important to emphasise in light of the earlier research on residential institutions that strong cultures were not necessarily damaging. Staff could benefit from the insights and practical help offered by positive peer support and effective managers were able to exploit this strength, along with training and supervision, to further the work of the home. Child cultures were more difficult to manage but could complement the work of staff, provided the children understood the aims of the establishment and how they were implemented and believed senior staff to have the capacity to achieve something on their behalf.

When the effects of these different patterns were assessed, it was found that the relationships between structure, staff cultures and child cultures influenced both outcomes for the homes and outcomes for children. The degree of concordance was associated with the home's response to change and the likelihood of continuing improvement. Where there was discord the opposite happened. It was also found that where these conditions applied, the children's home was of a high quality or a 'good' home in terms of the criteria employed in the Sinclair and Gibbs study. When the individual children were studied, the results were less clear but those who did best were in the higher quality homes, that is those where there were clear plans for children and 'drift' was prevented by continually revising services in the light of children's changing needs.

The study sets out a four stage process designed to help managers to:

• establish residential services that, in combination with other Part III provision, meet the needs of children being looked after in a locality
• set out the formal and belief goals for each residential home so that they meet identified needs and are concordant with societal goals for children in need
• establish a staff and child culture which complements the structure of a home
• put in place procedures to monitor the home's performance.

7 Private Children's Homes
Ian Gibbs, Ian Sinclair, *University of York*

The rapid growth in the number of private children's homes in recent years reflects general pressures on social services departments to consider using private provision as well as their own and the great reduction in the number of residential places provided by local authorities.

In 1996 official statistics for England recorded 202 private registered homes with places for nearly 1,500 young people in total. Published research on these homes has been limited: a pioneering descriptive study of three in the early 1980s by Berridge, a comparison by Knapp in the 1980s between their fees and the cost of public care, and a study of staffing carried out for the Warner committee. Thus it is not known whether the desire for profit has driven down the quality of care in homes as their detractors fear or, as their proponents believe, the discipline of the market and the energy of the entrepreneur have raised standards.

This study compares the clientele and other characteristics of eight private children's homes with local authority counterparts. Particular attention is paid to the issues facing managers.

The purpose of the study was to describe the clientele and other characteristics of a small sample of children's homes, to analyse the issues facing their managers and to compare the homes with the sample of local authority ones which the researchers had already studied in their project, *Children's Homes: A study in Diversity*.

Fifteen proprietors were approached. Ten agreed to participate and eight private homes were recruited to the study, all of them in or around London. The heads of the eight were interviewed, as were 49 residents, and postal questionnaires were sent to parents and social workers. Thirty parents and 26 social workers responded. The research instruments used were as far as possible the same as those used in the study of local authority homes so that results could be compared.

The heads mentioned a number of problems that were not shared by their local authority colleagues and seemed to stem from their position outside the local authority structure. The difficulties included: ensuring the prompt payment of fees; the need to relate to different local authorities with a variety of expectations; the problem, as they saw it, of accessing local authority services, particularly the education service; the awkwardness of having to balance professional and financial considerations, particularly, perhaps, if they were employed as a professional by a business organisation.

There were striking differences between the homes in the private and public sector in relation to:
- the distance between the young person's home or family and the home (residents in private homes were placed at a much greater distance from their neighbourhoods)
- the provision of education on the premises (much more likely in the private sector)
- the emphasis on treatment (homes in the private sector were more likely to describe themselves as having a therapeutic purpose and social workers were much more likely to say that the young people had been sent for treatment; conversely they were less likely to say that the purpose was preparation for independence)
- the role of the staff, who were much more likely to be involved in care planning and after-care if they were in the local authority sector.

These dissimilarities were accompanied by differences in the characteristics of residents and in the reaction of staff and residents to the homes. For example, in both sectors the majority of residents were teenagers. Residents in private homes were much more likely than those in local authority ones to be described by their social workers as displaying a variety of difficult behaviours (eg running away, delinquency, violence and sexual behaviour putting themselves or others at risk). Residents in private homes had less frequent contact with their families and were much less well informed about the plans for their future (eg about where they would go and when) and less likely to be happy about these plans.

Conversely residents in private homes were much more positive about their education, much more likely to be so about what the home was doing for them, and much less likely to say that they had been subjected to attempted bullying or sexual harassment, or to have been offered drugs.

Staff in the private sector were much more likely to say that the expectations of them were clear in various respects, were more likely to say that they had no concerns over keeping order and, on average, more satisfied with their work. Senior and experienced staff were particularly satisfied in the private sector and particularly dissatisfied in the local authority one.

In general the private homes seemed to the researchers to be more like the residential homes of the past. Their greater distance from the young people's homes and the inclusion of education on the premises made it easier for them to specify their aims and keep reasonable control of residents who were more dependent on them. Their disadvantages were that they were more isolated from the young people's families, and the young people themselves, while more likely to feel that the homes were doing them 'good', were less likely to be clear about what was being planned for them and more likely to wish they were in another residential home.

8 A Life Without Problems? The achievements of a therapeutic community
Michael Little, Siobhan Kelly, *Dartington Social Research Unit*

The study is an evaluation of the work of the Caldecott Community, a residential therapeutic centre in Kent. Analysis of children's needs and the results of follow-up studies are supplemented by autobiographical writing, in particular the diaries of one of the residents, 'Siobhan Kelly'. Siobhan's account and those of the other children illustrate daily life at Caldecott and help to explain how past disruption and trauma impinge upon their hopes and aspirations.

When the history of the Community was mapped out (it was founded in 1911) and the contribution of distinguished practitioners involved in its development assessed, it was found that there had been a major change over the last 25 years from a pragmatic approach designed to promote children's emotional security to a full-blown therapeutic strategy. For example, in 1950 there were 120 children and 40 staff, by 1995 there were 80 children and 150 adults who provided care in small family group units. The shift has led to a change in the characteristics of the children admitted, from unhappy but clever children privately referred to young people with serious behaviour difficulties and traumatic histories.

This research comprised longitudinal studies of three groups: the 60 children who left Caldecott between 1986 and 1990; eight who entered in 1990, and a matched group who underwent the selection process but were not admitted. The progress of all of them was followed up for at least two years. Most of those admitted were of primary school age but already presented complex problems. However, the range of their educational ability was significantly higher than that normally associated with disadvantaged children in residential homes.

Four characteristic home or background environments were identified: fragmented families; experiences of chronic sexual abuse; serious behaviour

This study evaluates the work of the therapeutic community at Caldecott. It explores the changing role of specialist residential provision and follows up the progress of leavers for two years. Outcomes are assessed for children with different needs.

difficulties; and long-term protection needs. The outcomes for young people in each group were charted two years after leaving.

The 21 children from fragmented families had the most limited family resources and it was not surprising that eight of them remained at Caldecott beyond statutory school leaving age, when they moved into flats and bedsits. The prognosis was usually good. However, seven experienced a placement breakdown before their sixteenth birthday and went on to further substitute care. For them the prognosis was less favourable, a prediction borne out by the fact that they tended to lose touch with families and become isolated. The remaining six returned to their families before the age of sixteen. Their circumstances were stable and long-term outcomes were quite good.

The group of sexually abused children comprised three boys and six girls. The departure of the girls from Caldecott was likely to be expedited by their highly sexualised behaviour. Three became pregnant during the follow up period but, while their school work was disrupted, they and two other girls who returned home to non-abusing parents or to substitute care coped reasonably well, as did the remaining girl who remained at Caldecott until she was 18. One of the boys, severely traumatised by abuse, continued to have psychiatric treatment well into adulthood. Of the other two, one returned home and the other went to substitute care where he eventually achieved a measure of stability.

The 20 with behavioural difficulties tended to be older on admission and to stay for a shorter period of time. Two thirds left before the age of 14, often as a result of family pressure on education authorities and sometimes contrary to advice from Caldecott staff. Four of them experienced further family breakdown and, like the three who went from Caldecott directly into residential care, found it difficult to manage independently. Their behaviour continued to be disturbed. The nine who went home did reasonably well and their presenting problems diminished. The remaining four, who stayed longest at Caldecott, made a smooth transition to employment from school.

Ten children from chaotic, inadequate and neglectful families were already regarded as long-term protection cases by the time they arrived. The prognosis was generally poor. Only two stayed at Caldecott until their late teens and only one succeeded in living independently. Of the others, one found a stable placement away from home while the remainder either became rootless and homeless or offended sufficiently seriously to enter custody or secure accommodation.

The findings drew attention to the importance of the stability and emotional warmth Caldecott provided and the significance for all looked after children of the period between their fifteenth and sixteenth birthdays. Without this help, the prognosis for many was worrying and behaviour problems were highly likely to recur. Caldecott seemed relatively good at giving young people a start in life compared with children in other residential settings. Leavers were four times more likely to find employment, three times less likely to be convicted or to enter custody and to have slightly better chances of establishing their own home.

The care staff at Caldecott had an average length of service of two years. Turnover was high and only a few saw their long-term future there. Continu-

A resident in the 1950s remembers the Caldecott Charter and Leila Rendel chanting at the beginning of every term:

This household is a Community and the members of this household are...
after which the names of all children and staff would be read out.

The term 'therapeutic community' is not one that Leila Rendel would have recognised, but she would have been in tune with the search for a treatment philosophy. She would also recognise the importance attached to education and acknowledge the enduring charge of elitism.

ity for the children was, therefore, more likely to be provided by domestic and maintenance staff or by managers and teachers than by care workers. Nevertheless, the carers were an optimistic group. Few felt unequal to the work and most believed that any uncertainties could be overcome by training and experience. But while this unusual degree of vitality was maintained, they were often emotionally drained by their work. They might not stay long in the job but brought considerable commitment to the task for as long as their energy lasted.

The Caldecott Community was considered to be in a good position to make fine judgements about how best to look after vulnerable children in residential care and to ensure the best possible outcomes for them. Its stress on education, its egalitarian attitudes, its use of psycho-dynamic therapy and the willingness to welcome and support former residents provided a good example from which others might learn.

Its weaknesses were found to lie in its failure to engage sufficiently with young people's families and home communities, in its weak links with local social services and its reluctance to share mutual expertise with other residential education provision.

9 Children's Homes: A study in diversity

Ian Sinclair, Ian Gibbs, *University of York*

Too many children's homes have recently found themselves at the centre of scandals arising from the behaviour of the residents or staff. Yet many apparently similar establishments seem to continue do unobtrusive good work. Can these differences in the apparent outcomes of homes be explained? And if so, how much has the explanation to do with variations in resources? Studies in the 1960s and 1970s suggested that there are explanations for such variations and that resources are certainly not the whole answer. This was the background that led to the research described below.

The study aimed:
- to document variations between current children's homes in their immediate and longer term outcomes
- to explain these varying outcomes by relating them to the characteristics of the residents, the 'structural' features of the homes (eg their size and staffing ratios) and the homes' regimes.

The investigation focused on 48 children's homes in five authorities. Information about the homes was drawn from postal questionnaires dealing with regimes, brief details about the characteristics and behaviour of approximately 1,200 residents in the homes over the previous year, and from the ratings of research interviewers.

Information concerning the staff was the result of guided interviews with heads, data on staffing ratios, qualifications and turnover, and postal questionnaires completed by about 300 individuals.

Information concerning residents and families was gleaned from

This study assesses the quality of care in children's homes and the factors associated with it. The impact of differences in quality on the homes themselves, the staff and the resident young people are explored.

The ideas behind the study derive partly from research on residential care in the 1960s which highlighted the impact of current environment on the behaviour of young people. However, it is also influenced by more recent concerns with the paths through life taken by disadvantaged young people and the reasons why they diverge.

interviews with 223 residents, and 99 parents, and from postal question-naires completed by 176 social workers. Follow-up information was sought from residents and social workers approximately nine months later.

This data was used to describe the homes and their residents, to develop measures of outcome and to explain outcomes in terms of the characteristics of the homes and their residents.

Homes varied in size from 4 to 20 beds but were most commonly small (6 beds), 'general purpose', (although specialisation did exist) and reasonably permissive. Staffing ratios were on average 60 hours per week per place (a figure which varied from 23 to 141). Resident turnover was high (six out of ten left within two months), although around one in seven stayed for at least six months. At any one time these longer staying residents took up around half the beds.

Heads of homes were often able to give impressive accounts of how they tried to achieve certain aims (eg improve health or schooling). They were commonly bothered by lack of autonomy, problems consequent on reorgani-sation, and the unclear or conflicting remits of their homes. Heads who experienced problems in one of these areas were more likely to do so in the others.

Staff other than heads were very rarely trained but were experienced– two thirds had been in post for three years or more. They considered them-selves deeply involved with showing concern for the young people, keeping order and general supervision but they wished they were more involved with therapeutic work and after care. Satisfaction came from a sense of a clear role, good support from colleagues and management, adequate pay, security and job prospects, and a sense that residents were making progress. Morale was more likely to be good if the member of staff received regular supervi-sion, had a role which involved care planning or after-care, and was relatively new to residential work. Staff morale varied considerably between homes.

Almost all residents were aged between 12 and 17. In the eyes of their social workers, less than one in six came from families where both their natural parents were living, seven out of ten had been excluded from school or frequently truanted, six out of ten had at least some involvement in delinquency and three or more out of ten had been violent to adults, violent to other children, run away from 'care', run away from their own homes, put themselves or others at risk through sexual behaviour and harmed them-selves or attempted suicide.

Generally they were first looked after in their teens because they had fallen out with their families, but minorities did so because of abuse, or behaviour outside the home. The purposes of placement were variously short-term (eg to allow assessment or a breathing space), medium term (eg to prepare for independence or another placement) or to allow for long-term upbringing. Residential care was preferred to fostering because of the young people's choices or because the residents were seen as too difficult for fostering.

Nearly a third of school age young people were not in school (although there were variations between homes and one authority had been particu-larly successful in re-establishing school attendance). Six out of ten of those

The project was mounted in a context where it was unclear what the homes were supposed to do. This uncertainty of purpose, the high costs of the homes, their vulnerability to scandal, critical research and professional views of good practice all raised questions over whether the homes should survive.

Overall, these findings raised vital questions about the effect of the variations that were documented. One might ask for example what are the implications of having a high staff child ratio, and what difference it makes if there is a relatively high proportion of trained staff.

who had left school were neither employed nor receiving training. Among those who stayed six months or more roughly three quarters of those with a previous conviction and four in ten of those without one received a caution or criminal conviction while in the home. Large variations between homes in delinquency and running away rates were not fully explained by intake.

Residents appraised residential care in terms of whether they had wished to be looked after, whether the home was a reasonable place in which to live, whether there was a purpose in being there, whether they moved on at 'the right time' and the quality of their life on leaving. Roughly a third had not wished to enter 'care', a third had mixed feelings about this and a third were in favour of it. Given that they were in care, they were much more likely to prefer residential care to foster care.

In general, residents appreciated homes where they were not bullied, sexually harassed or led into trouble, and where the staff listened, there was a reasonable regime and the other residents were friendly. They particularly valued it if they felt they had changed, settled down or made some tangible improvement (eg in education).

The young people were critical if they felt they were moved on before they were ready and around a quarter wanted continuing contact with staff (which they rarely had). The great majority wanted to be in frequent touch with their families but not to live with them. Around half were seriously mistaken about social work plans for them (eg about where they were expected to go). Many who had left had lonely and rather frightening lives.

Most parents welcomed the break produced by the young person's removal to 'care', seeing it as the resolution of an intolerable family situation. On the whole they saw the effects as positive, feeling that the young people calmed down and that absence made the heart grow fonder. Drawbacks, if any, were the sadness of separation and the corrupting influence of delinquent peers. Generally they wanted the younger residents to return home in due course but were more likely to accept that the older ones would not do so. The research considered three main outcomes:

- *The social environment of the home* Homes in which the young people were more likely to behave delinquently also tended to be seen by residents and staff as marked by difficult behaviour and unfriendly relationships between the residents. In these homes residents tended to feel they had little say in how the home was run, that being in the home was a waste of time and that they were not being helped. Staff morale was typically low and the quality of relationships they had with young people was poor. The project was able to measure the degree to which the homes conformed to this turbulent model.
- *Individual misery* Four out of ten residents had considered killing themselves in the previous month. The project used this and other information to measure the misery of individual residents at two points.
- *Adjustment* The project used social worker ratings derived from *Looking after Children* to measure the adjustment of residents at two points and over a range of dimensions (eg schooling, family relationships).

When the relationship between these outcomes was explored, it was found that difficult social environments were not related to measures of the

Residential homes need to be evaluated against three very different criteria. The first is their success in responding to short-term emergencies, the second is their capacity to provide a time for reflection and perhaps for treatment and the third is their success in providing a stable, homely environment in which young people can live for some time. A key issue concerns the degree to which these purposes can be handled successfully in the same home.

previous delinquency or disturbance of the residents, to staffing ratios, the proportion of trained staff or to whether the head was trained. Homes were, however, more likely to do well:

- if they were small
- if the head of home felt that roles were clear, mutually compatible and not disturbed by reorganisation and that he or she had adequate autonomy
- if the staff agreed how the home should run.

Individual misery was related to experience of attempted bullying or sexual harassment, missing family or friends, relationships with the resident group, previous experience of bullying or sexual harassment, and (in a reverse direction) a feeling of success in social roles (eg of being good at a sport). This suggests that policy and practice should encourage the resident in their successes, pay close attention to their relationships with other residents and include sensitivity to loss and attention to previous abuse.

Changes in adjustment were generally small and could be eroded on discharge to a new environment. Change was more likely to be positive where:

- the head of home had a coherent philosophy of how change could be enabled in particular areas
- the turnover was not great.

The findings suggest that Social Services Departments should aim to:

- keep their homes as small as possible
- appoint heads who have a clear philosophy, are agreed with the management on the way the home should run, are sensitive to the deeply felt concerns of residents and are capable of uniting the staff group behind them
- encourage contact with family but remain sensitive to the wish of many residents to stay in contact with their families but not to live with them.

High staffing ratios and high proportions of qualified staff were not shown to affect performance. They are probably less important than adequate preventive work before admission, an ability to handle discharge at the residents' own pace and adequate after-care.

10 Working in Children's Homes: Challenges and complexities

Dorothy Whitaker, Lesley Archer, Leslie Hicks, *University of York*

It has long been known that working in residential homes for children is emotionally demanding and peculiarly stressful. Staff work in groups inside a larger, often hierarchical organisation surrounded by wider networks. Subgroup, inter-group and culture dynamics therefore become important. This study explores what takes place in children's homes, taking as a relatively unusual starting point the views and reported experiences of the staff.

The research consisted of two inter-linking pieces of qualitative work. In the first, the research team carried out a series of in-depth telephone inter-

This study explores the experiences of staff working in children's homes. It uses the model of 'working life space' to show the people and organisations with whom staff groups must interact and 'force field analysis' to chart the factors that facilitate or impede good practice and good outcomes.

views with unit managers from 39 homes in 13 local authorities. The interviews elicited unit managers' accounts of difficult practice situations, concentrating on the distinctions between those that had been resolved and those that had not worked out as they would have wished.

In the second study, visits were made to six children's homes, two in each of three local authorities, at about monthly intervals over the course of 15 months. A university-based researcher was paired with a practitioner-researcher seconded from the local authority, and both listened to staff talking about their work. An action research model was introduced to each staff team. Devised by Kurt Lewin, it involved successively setting a goal, making a plan, taking action and reflecting on the consequences of putting the plan into action. Where staff groups could not adhere to this model, much was learned about what interfered with planning and taking action, what distracted staff from the pursuit of goals, what displaced time to reflect, and the like. Notes were kept of the sessions and each set of notes was taken back to the unit at the next visit for staff to check and discuss. Staff comments on the notes were recorded.

The team used information from both studies to construct a picture of the tasks staff carried out in relation to their overall goal of benefiting the children and young people in their care. The tasks fell into five main areas: working with individual children and young people, working with the mix of young people, working within the larger organisation, working with the networks surrounding each young person and the home, and maintaining the staff group as a viable team.

The data also showed sources of reward and stress and the factors that seemed to influence alternations between good and bad patches. Changes occurred rapidly in the children's homes. Young people came and went frequently, new short-term goals emerged, unanticipated events or emergency situations occurred. Practice was shown to be highly susceptible to rapid change and the resulting adjustment of priorities.

Successful handling of such a volatile environment relied partly on staff developing patterns of working that could remain consistent in the face of change. Much energy was devoted to developing and maintaining a viable and effective team to which they could turn for emotional and practical support. There were occasions when a perceived lack of understanding, whether from the head of the unit or among co-workers or from external managers, could be detrimental to the morale of the entire staff group.

Threats to the viability of the staff group might arise internally through personnel changes or from new mixes in the composition of the group of young people, or externally, as a result of school exclusions, unsympathetic neighbours, or new departmental policies. The research showed that where problems occurred, simplistic explanations on the part of any of those concerned obscured realities and complexities. If 'explanations' involved blaming one person or a group of people, they were likely to be a barrier to understanding what needed to be done to restore equilibrium.

The researchers identified characteristics of good practice in the five main areas. They used Kurt Lewin's force field model to display the factors which facilitated or hindered good practice inside and outside the home and

In pursuing their overall goal of benefiting the children and young people in their care, staff groups have to work in five main areas. They must: (a) plan for and work with individual young people; (b) work with the group of young people; (c) work with, and be managed by, the Social Services Department; (d) work with other people and organisations outside the home and (e) work to develop and maintain themselves as a viable and effective team.

Sources of reward included feeling the support of a strong staff team, seeing that the young people in one's care actually benefited, feeling that difficult situations could be handled competently by self and/or colleagues, and feeling valued by departmental colleagues and managers.

Sources of stress include being faced by a pile-up of tasks, being aware that it was impossible to stay in control of all the situations which might arise; being at the receiving end of abuse from the young people; knowing that the unexpected and the unmanageable might occur at any time; feeling helpless or potentially helpless in the face of events; feeling vulnerable to blame if things went wrong; and lacking the sense of any support or confidence from management.

Key influences on culture were the rate of turnover of the young people, the proportion of emergency placements, the mix of young people, the number of young people not in school, the stability of membership in the staff group, the composition of both young people and staff with respect to gender and race, how secure or not the staff felt within its own organisation, the presence or absence of conflict with managers, and the level of morale.

which facilitated or hindered good outcomes for the young people. It was possible to distinguish between homes that were well placed or poorly placed to carry out good practice.

With respect to the cultures which they developed, staff groups were found to have much in common. They espoused the same overall goal of benefiting each young person, they faced the same range of tasks, and they shared many of the same values. Yet each group developed a unique culture with respect to the details of its goal systems; its beliefs and attitudes; norms, structures, procedures, routines and customs; degree of internal cohesiveness, and the nature of the boundary between the home and the outside world. In each case the distinctive culture that emerged was influenced by the specific circumstances the group faced, the leadership style of the unit manager and relationships within the staff group. Some staff groups were mutually supportive, some conflict-ridden. Some were secure and competent, some insecure and less competent. The researchers noted that, in extremity, some staff groups were so divided or fragmented that they could not be said to have a distinct culture.

Using this extensive portrayal of how staff felt, thought and operated within residential child care, the researchers outlined the knowledge-base, practice skills and personal qualities required to work in this sphere. The knowledge base included an understanding of personal development, transgenerational processes and family dynamics, the positive and negative potentials of group living, networks and network interactions, and organisational structures and dynamics. Necessary skills included a range of listening, observing, intervening and assessment competencies, in order to understand emotional reactions and feelings in the young people and in themselves, and to work effectively across the whole range of tasks. The researchers enumerated the personal qualities of those who are able to cope and sustain themselves within the demands of the job and the qualities of those who are not suitable for this type of work.

There is no list of circumstances under which residential care should be a preferred option. However, the research suggested it was preferable when there was a deficit in attachment-forming capacity and a young person could profit from having available a range of carers; when he or she had a history of having abused other children; when he or she felt threatened by the prospect of living in a family or needed respite from it; when multiple potential adult attachment figures might forestall a young person from emotionally abandoning his or her own parent(s); when the emotional load of caring for a very disturbed or chaotic young person was best distributed among a number of adult carers; when the young person preferred residential care to any form of family care and would sabotage family care if it was provided.

11 Evaluating Residential Care Training: Towards qualified leadership

Dione Hills, Camilla Child, Julie Hills, Vicky Blackburn, *Tavistock Institute*

The Residential Child Care Initiative (RCCI) was set up by the Department of Health in response to the crises in residential child care in the 1980s and amid concern about the small proportion of qualified senior staff in the sector. Between 1992 and 1997, the initiative provided eight DipSW programmes with additional funding to enhance their programmes and local authorities received funding to second senior staff to DipSW programmes.

Evaluation was designed to establish how far the DipSW programmes had met the needs of the students seconded, their employers, and the other 'stakeholders' in the initiative. It also sought to compare the designated and non-designated programmes in terms of content, satisfaction and outcome

This study evaluates a training initiative designed to improve the knowledge and experience of senior staff in residential care seconded to DipSW courses. It explores the views of participants, their managers and colleagues and follows the secondees as they return to work to see how far they are able to practise new ideas.

and to examine the impact of the programme at a local authority and service level. It made use of a variety of methods including a survey of all staff seconded under the initiative, a systematic comparison between the designated programmes and a selection of six others run by DipSW, as well as case studies in six local authorities, chosen on the basis of regional and organisational diversity. Seconded staff, colleagues, managers and trainers were interviewed in the case study authorities. The team also examined national statistics to see how far the initiative had contributed to an increase in the overall proportion of qualified staff within the sector.

National figures (from the LGMB/ADSS staff survey) indicated that there was a considerable increase in the proportion of qualified residential staff in managerial positions during the years of the initiative. However, part of the increase had to be attributed to the reduction in size in the sector and the qualification bar to unit manager posts that most authorities introduced during this period. RCCI appears to have had a role in counteracting the loss of qualified staff during the closure of units in the late 1980s/early 1990s.

Prior to the initiative, there were fears that senior residential staff obtaining a DipSW would use it as an opportunity to leave the sector. However, the staff survey did not suggest that this was happening to any extent: 77 of the 89 respondents who returned to work after completing their programme returned to residential care and 64% indicated an intention to remain there for the foreseeable future. Of those who moved out, several had been forced to do so by the restructuring of services and most were still working in closely related areas, such as community support teams, inspection units or foster care support. Of those who expressed an intention to move out of residential work, most gave poor career prospects as the reason, coupled with low status, unsatisfactory terms and working conditions and frustrations arising from shift work and lack of professional autonomy.

Three quarters of the secondees attended designated RCCI centres and a quarter regular DipSW programmes. The participating programmes had used the extra funding to reorganise. Most had introduced a special 'pathway' for residential child care students within their overall programme, usually during the second year. They also appointed specialist lecturers, who generally acted as residential care 'champions', taught the specialist modules and sometimes led tutorial groups for RCCI students.

Overall, the study found the DipSW to be a relevant qualification because of the attention it paid to the professional development of reflective practitioners. However, a number of relevant areas sometimes overlooked on DipSW programmes were identified by 'stakeholders', who included students, social work trainers, CCETSW, social services managers and other agencies (including the Department of Health). They were:

- *under the heading of knowledge and values,* questions of assessment, child protection and anti-discriminatory practice
- *under the heading of management,* the management of residential units and the problems of coping with the mix of children
- *under the heading of practice issues,* communication skills, the management of challenging behaviour, handling restraint in a group setting and addressing young people's health and educational needs.

There were limitations in all programmes in the extent to which these issues were addressed in ways relevant to residential care. More efforts were made on the designated RCCI programmes and on non-RCCI programmes where a special residential care tutor had been employed or residential care modules provided. Although management per se is not included in DipSW programmes, some programmes found creative ways to incorporate aspects of management into the specialist pathways, for example, by teaching a module from a specifically 'management' perspective. Communication skills often focused on younger children rather than adolescents, which were the group with which the secondees were generally more concerned. Moreover, issues to do with restraint and challenging behaviour were regarded as being the responsibility of local authorities rather than DipSW programmes. The teaching of topics related to health and education was often very limited.

Even if these topics were covered quite adequately on the specialist residential care pathways, there remained a particular concern that most were neglected on the general modules of most programmes, which often failed to relate general theory to specific practice examples. There was often a shortage of positive and realistic inputs about what good residential care could achieve, when such an explanation would have been relevant not only to students wishing to work in residential care but also to field workers making decisions about young people's placement.

Students attending the courses spoke well of the theoretical content of their courses, and rated it as the most important element in terms of their initial expectations. RCCI programmes were rated somewhat higher than non-RCCI in terms of satisfaction with theory teaching and practice skills, although this result was not statistically significant. However, levels of satisfaction in terms of how residential care was represented in course materials and the level of knowledge of, and commitment to, the sector were significantly greater in RCCI programmes. Students particularly valued the involvement of outside lecturers with expertise in the field. However, the type of course attended seemed to make little difference to the outcome in terms of continued commitment to residential care. Eleven of the 12 who left the sector had qualified through RCCI programmes.

The survey findings accorded with the results obtained from interviews with secondees, their managers and local authority colleagues. Both studies indicated that secondment had given senior residential care staff greater self confidence, largely because they now had a better understanding of theory to back up their work. Since most had experience and skill before they started their courses, the programmes did not add much to their basic competence, although the training sometimes gave them new skills to draw upon and a sense of enhanced status and authority.

Several respondents said the course had improved their managerial skills, particularly their ability to think strategically, to conceptualise the work of their unit and to lead and supervise, staff. Similarly, some of the staff group said the secondees had developed a more positive view of training and some had gone out of their way to pass their new learning on, either through running activities themselves or through one-to-one support and mentoring of colleagues.

'The main thing the DipSW did was to give me confidence. I had always thought that I would like to do such and such a thing, but was never sure if I was right. The context of the course validated many things for me. Now I can tell people with authority'. *(returning deputy)*

'He thought the DipSW has given him a better idea of planning, a more strategic view of the organisations, and planning of services.' *(staff member)*

'I noticed she was sharing much more knowledge that she had from being at college. That willingness to come forward and share that information helped me... it seems to have given her greater insight into the families she worked with, ways of unpacking the problem and deciding how to deal with it.' *(staff member)*

Not all the secondees were able to influence how their unit worked, although 74% indicated they had been able to make changes to their practice. Evidence from units in the case study authorities included the introduction of key working, new supervisory arrangements and greater collaborative work with other agencies. Inevitably, some had faced opposition from colleagues and managers, rather highlighting a lack of support for returning staff, who often faced an unenviable mixture of high expectation and poor supervision.

Senior managers were circumspect about permitting the Initiative to have an impact on the residential provision for which they were responsible. All the case study authorities had been through a period of considerable change in relation to the residential services they provided. In this context, the Initiative had to be regarded as a 'small drop in the ocean', although some local authorities did more than others to use the secondments strategically. However, while senior managers were looking for unit officers with well developed managerial skills, it had not been the central focus of the programmes to provide them. This suggested a degree of confusion concerning the skills and competencies required for senior residential staff roles, which reflected a wider uncertainty about the appropriate role and purpose of residential care within the spectrum of services.

In four of the six authorities, the availability of RCCI appeared to have an influence on the attitudes of senior managers and training sections to the secondment of residential care staff to qualification training, although national statistics suggest that the majority of authorities were in the process of reducing the number of secondments or of ending them altogether. This suggests that there continues to be a large group of experienced residential workers who are unable to obtain secondment on to DipSW courses, despite the fact that most authorities are now introducing a qualification bar to unit officer posts. Most authorities were exploring more 'low cost' solutions to the training of residential child care workers, including work-based routes, part time courses and NVQs.

The Initiative came to an end at a time when programmes and local authorities were expressing considerable concern about the future of training for residential child care staff. Colleges no longer have the additional funding for specialist course inputs, although most of the RCCI colleges say they will make efforts to continue with enhanced training for residential child care workers.

12 The External Management of Children's Homes by Local Authorities

Richard Whipp, Ian Kirkpatrick, Martin Kitchener, Dianne Owen, *Cardiff University Business School*

Several reports and inquiries into residential care for children have highlighted management difficulties. Managers of homes are often isolated from mainstream child-care and feel beleaguered when difficulties arise in their homes. External line management can also be problematic: some senior managers in local authorities have no experience of residential work and responsibility for community homes (they may manage several establishments) is often one duty among many. It was thought likely to be helpful, therefore, if researchers from the management field were to examine this aspect of residential homes.

This study, commissioned later than the others, examines the models employed by social services departments for managing children's homes. Particular attention is paid to the effects of different types of external management on staff behaviour and attitudes and the working of homes generally.

The project aimed to analyse the models of management employed in a sample of metropolitan, shire, London, and unitary social services departments, and to see how these impacted on the external management of children's homes. Models were therefore evaluated for their appropriateness. Techniques for monitoring performance and remedial intervention were discussed and a framework known to be useful in the context of the public sector was applied to determine what constitutes effective practice.

Another aim was to develop a framework for understanding and identifying 'best practice'. To do so, an 'inclusive' approach was adopted. The study was not limited to assessing the more obvious aspects of external management, such as the ways in which homes were controlled and inspected by line managers, support services and inspection teams. In addition, the study included relationships between residential workers and fieldwork teams (the impact of care plans and child placement decisions) and the question of how far care workers were an integrated part of wider departmental strategies. The inclusive approach also meant looking at the external management of child placements made 'out of area', in children's homes run by the independent sector. Evidence came from a comparative study of twelve local authorities in England and Wales, including a mix of metropolitan boroughs, shire counties, London boroughs and unitary authorities. Sources of information included interviews, non-participant observation and a variety of archival and secondary data.

The authorities participating in the study were all large 'users' of residential care. There were, however, significant differences between them, some being large providers, for example, a shire county with over forty homes, and others relying almost exclusively on placements in the independent sector. In all cases, there had been a steady down-sizing of residential provision over the last decade, often without resources being transferred into alternative forms of substitute care. In some authorities this had resulted in low vacancy rates in the remaining homes, a tendency for unplanned emergency placements and 'distress purchasing' from the independent sector. Almost all authorities had encountered problems of overspending on out-of-area budgets.

The sample authorities varied in terms of how their children's services were organised. The majority had a client split between children and adult services with considerable specialisation. In the large shire counties and one metropolitan there was also a geographical split between divisions, although, in two cases, the divide had been replaced by greater centralisation. A number of authorities had experimented with purchaser/provider splits in children's services, although this often amounted to little more than a re-labelling exercise. In the majority of cases, there existed a traditional functional split between 'in house' resources (children's and family placement) and field social work teams. Many departments had engaged in some kind of internal review of residential services, often leading to increased expenditure on staff training and to attempts to develop greater specialisation of children's homes with explicit statements of purpose and function.

The research concluded that the management of residential services had to be understood in the context of a professional bureaucracy. Looked after children relied on several professional groups, each of which was largely independent, self-organised and trained outside the agency for whom they worked. Practitioners paradoxically enjoyed a high degree of autonomy in their work. Furthermore, despite the aspiration to a flexible structure designed round the needs of children, hierarchies in professional bureaucracies like the social services department were as likely to reflect professional status as chains of command.

The findings revealed a variety of management practices both within and between local authorities. Nowhere was this more evident than with the direct line management and control of homes. There were marked differences in the span of control of line managers, a fact which influenced the amount of time and effort managers were able to devote to supervision. Differences in management style were also noted, with some managers adopting a 'hands-on' approach–maintaining regular contact with homes and intervention in operational matters–and others, a more 'hands-off' style. Depending on the context, a 'hands-off' approach was viewed either as positive, allowing the officer in charge much greater autonomy, or negative, resulting in the greater isolation of the home from the department. Not surprisingly, the credibility of line managers with home staff was found to be greatly enhanced if they had previous experience in residential care. In about half the cases, a problem of children's homes becoming increasingly isolated was recognised, with some attempts made to draw unit managers into wider decision-making processes through joint training sessions, placement meetings, multi-functional project groups and strategic workshops. In some local authorities, a delegation of responsibility for budgets from line manager to officer in charge had occurred. While not always liked, this move had the advantage of allowing officers much greater flexibility to link spending decisions more closely to the particular needs of the resident group, for example, in the allocation of over-time hours and the purchasing of food and materials.

The inspection of children's homes to ensure compliance with statutory regulations had been given much greater emphasis in all the local authorities studied. Here too however, there were variations in practice, especially with monthly Regulation 22 visits. In some cases, senior management had devoted resources to ensuring visits were regularly conducted by staff not associated with the home and that information was collated and referred upwards. In others, it was clear that Regulation 22 visits were infrequent, conducted by the line managers of homes and that little information was passed on to higher managers. Generally speaking, arms-length inspections were better organised, although there were sharp contrasts between authorities where the emphasis was on legal compliance and those where inspection was also viewed as an opportunity for development and the continuous improvement of the service. The latter built feedback into their visits and ensure their findings informed policy and training.

The satisfactory placement of children was a continual problem. In many departments, a large number of placements were unplanned and only loosely based on need. The extent of this was determined in part, by the size of the residential sector (the number of beds available), the availability of

Throughout England and Wales the number of 'out of area' placements in independent sector children's homes has dramatically increased. There are, however, important differences in the way these placements are managed, particularly between London and non-London authorities. London boroughs tended to make greater use of external placements and had developed a shared data base to compare information about the standard and quality of independent providers. Key differences existed between local authorities which had invested in contract management roles and systematic monitoring and those where these activities were under-developed. The majority of placements were spot purchases, although some local authorities had developed longer term relationships with providers (mainly voluntary) through block contracts.

foster placements and by the degree to which demand had been reduced through 'refocusing' and investment in preventative services. A common picture was a continuous process of bargaining and compromise between field social work teams under pressure to place children and resource managers keen to gate-keep this process in order to protect the specialist statements of purpose and function of children's homes. Various mechanisms were employed to try to ensure improved placement planning, including joint panels, liaison officers and short-stay family resource centres. While these structures helped in some cases to reduce the number of emergency placements, they also increased antagonism between residential field work teams and were routinely bypassed when senior managers were involved in crisis decisions. One outcome of this was a growing contradiction between official policies which aimed to increase the level of specialisation and clarity of goals in children's homes and the pragmatic concerns of fieldwork managers demanding quick access to placements.

The lack of specialist qualifications among residential staff had clearly begun to be addressed. The success of these efforts was heavily influenced by the orientation of the local authority to personnel and training. Two types emerged. The centralised, rule fixated approach and a more facilitating, advisory role. The second had proved more helpful in creating appropriate skills. Departments which had linked personal issues to strategic thinking appeared more able to address the problems of redeployment and re-training which needs-led decisions on specialisation require.

Contrasting profiles of strategic orientation in authorities emerged with a wide range of assumptions behind service planning. Historical legacies were an important influence and the degree of commitment to child residential care from the centre had a critical effect on staff working with children. Departments differed in their ability to think strategically in relation to residential care and especially in how they translated policies into practice. Levels of integration were central. There might be long-standing friction between different professional groups. Inter-agency and disciplinary liaisons required clearly defined tasks directed at improving child/residential care need. It emerged that departments differed in their capacity to acquire and use such knowledge, despite the wealth of experience available in the various professional groups. It was also the case that consultation and reflection ignored many who were skilled and informed, such as youth justice managers and out-of-hours teams.

'True for us' exercises

Three criticisms are frequently levelled at research. One is to do with timing, *What you say may have been true then, but it probably isn't now*. Another is about place, *What you say may be true there, but it probably doesn't apply here*. Or finally, *What you say may be true, but there's nothing we can do about it*. Such doubts make research less authoritative and limit its impact on policy and practice.

The following exercises provide a counter to such complaints by suggesting how professionals, managers and students can translate the research findings to their own situation and so test the value of the book. It is hoped that they will be found useful not only by those who have the time and the resources to apply them in training, management or practice. They work as well as a basis for reflection on the relationship between the broad sweep of the research studies and the circumstances of individual local authorities and neighbourhoods.

Twelve exercises are provided. They are organised around the five areas of residence considered in the overview essay:

The children	Exercises 1, 2, 3
The homes	4, 5, 6
The staff	7, 8
Management, inspection and training	9, 10
The wider context	11, 12.

The exercises have also been designed for the different groups of people involved in looking after children in residential care. Most are short and will take no more than an hour or two to complete. A few are more elaborate and may require the support of a specialised trainer. Many will require a fresh look at the case records of children for whom the participants are responsible and great care will be needed regarding the confidentiality of any information used. It is possible, too, that problems and unmet needs may be uncovered as a result of the exercises; if so, they must not be ignored and responsibility for taking action should be quickly determined.

Exercises 1, 3, 6 and 8 can be co-ordinated by the staff group in a residential centre, although they will want to involve one or two external people such as professionals working with the family and elected members.

Exercises 2, 5, 7, 9 and 10 are to be co-ordinated by the managers of homes, bringing in their staff, their line managers, elected members and other professionals as necessary.

Exercises 11 and 12 require a mixed group of professionals and members and are probably best co-ordinated by somebody outside the residential sector.

Exercise 4 is a half-day workshop for many people and best co-ordinated by a trainer.

Trainers are involved in Exercises 4 and 7. It is possible for a trainer to link all the exercises over an extended period, possibly to underpin a wider development exercise. This could be achieved through three parallel training programmes:

- one based on Exercises 1, 3, 6 and 8 and largely involving residential staff
- one based on Exercises 2, 5, 7, 9 and 10, largely involving managers
- one based on Exercises 11 and 12, mainly for wider groups of professionals.

The work could then be brought together in a single day seminar beginning with the half-day Exercise 4. The second part of the day might involve presentations about the research and the local authority response to recommendations emerging from the exercises. The participation of the Director of Social Services, all managers of residential care and representation by elected members would be essential.

1   What residential settings know about young people in their care

Basic information on children in need is an essential prerequisite for effective intervention. But important information is all too often not readily available or fails to be passed on. In the worst case this can undermine the protection of children placed in residential care.

AIM

The aim of this exercise is to help key staff in the homes to know what information is available on young people, what to collect at the point of referral and where to get it. It is best carried out by a small group of residential staff from a single children's home. It will help to invite a field social worker responsible for one of the current residents. The manager of the home can facilitate the exercise but need not participate.

PRELIMINARY TASKS

Photocopy for the participants summaries 2, 3 and 10. If the authority or agency uses *Looking After Children* materials, collect records for two children from the home or the field worker. If it does not, obtain blank *Looking After Children* Essential Information and (age appropriate) Assessment and Action Records and complete them using information from the record held in the home (allow an hour to do this).

THE EXERCISE

1 Work as a group. Spend no more than ten minutes each answering the following questions:
- What information was missing from the case record?
- What more is known about the child now than is written on the record?
- Is it clear from the information available to staff what plans have been made for working with the child and his or her family and by whom?
- Is there any information that might be available elsewhere that could contribute to the effectiveness of the plan?
- From where is this information best gathered and who should take responsibility for doing so?

2 What steps can the home and the field social worker take to ensure that in future useful information is exchanged
i)   at the point of referral
ii)   as the work progresses
iii) when the child moves on?

Who will take responsibility for ensuring that recommended action is considered by managers?

2   What can residential care achieve together with other services?

Residential care is best viewed in the context of children's needs and the range of services available to meet those needs. The range of available services is often known as the Part III continuum after that part of the *Children Act* 1989. The research shows that all residential care is dependent on the contribution of other services if it is to be effective in meeting the complex needs of children.

AIM

The aim of the exercise is to help managers of homes together with residential staff consider where their service fits within the continuum of services available in their local authority. It is best initiated and carried out by the manager of the home in close consultation with staff. An experienced professional from health or social services could act as a catalyst to thinking about what else is available.

PRELIMINARY TASKS

Be familiar with pages 17-18 of the overview essay. Assemble background papers on three children currently looked after in the children's home. Try to select a reasonably typical group of children.

THE EXERCISE

1 Divide into three equal groups, each taking one of the selected case records. Each group should make an assessment of needs of their case on the day he or she was admitted to the home. Do this by spending no more than ten minutes considering the child's needs in each of the following areas:
• living situation
• family and social relationships
• physical and mental health
• social and anti-social behaviour (including identity, social presentation and self care)
• education and employment.

2 Reconvene as a group. Spend ten minutes reading to each other the findings on each case. Highlight consistent themes. Write a paragraph on each theme. Take a ten minute break.

3 Look at the continuum described on page 14 of the overview essay. Add to it other services available in your local authority. Identify any gaps. Spend no more than 15 minutes on this task.

4 For the three children considered, spend ten minutes each answering the following questions:
• What contribution does your home make to each child's needs?
• What other services in your local authority continuum are appropriate for the three children? Are they used? If they are not used, identify the difficulties and obstacles.
• What other services currently unavailable in your local authority would contribute towards a satisfactory outcome?
Finally, spend five minutes considering who will take responsibility for ensuring that the findings from the exercise are considered by senior managers.

3   Being realistic about what can be achieved on behalf of children looked after in residential care

The research urges a general consideration of society's objectives for residential care. It is also helpful to be realistic about what can be achieved for each child looked after.

AIM

The aim of this exercise is to encourage residential workers to think about what the residential home can achieve on behalf of residents. It can be undertaken by any practitioner to consider one or more of the children for whom he or she is responsible. Where their age and development are appropriate the exercise can be done together with a looked after child. The method is as useful beyond residential care as it is within it. It would be productive if groups of professionals met to discuss the results.

PRELIMINARY TASKS

Read the concluding section of the overview essay, especially page 49. Select a closed case record, ideally from the place in which you work. If the exercise is undertaken at a seminar (in other words in a context where there is no case information readily available) practitioners may be able to rely on their memory of the last child they worked with.

THE EXERCISE

1 On one side of an A4 sheet of paper draw three columns of equal width:
write *needs* at the head of the first column
write *worst outcomes* in the second
write *best outcomes* in the third.
Draw five lines across the same sheet, again equally spaced
write *living situation* in the left-hand margin of the first row
family relations in the second row
social behaviour in the third
health in the fourth
education and employment in the fifth.
This will take you two minutes.

2 Select a long-term point for the outcome for your selected child, say two years from the present or the age of 18. Fill in the boxes on your sheet. Relate your expectations about outcomes to the child's needs, problems and abilities. Try to justify your judgements with some of the evidence described in the studies. This will take you about 30 minutes.

3 Spend another 30 minutes setting out those services which you think will achieve the best outcomes described for your case. Ask yourself whether these services are available and, if not, what can be done to bring gaps to the attention of managers. Again, be realistic but imaginative. Remember that you have a role as an advocate and champion for children for whom you have responsibility.

4   What can be expected of residential care in your local authority?

Good residential care has been shown to depend on clear definitions of its function and purpose. Such definitions need to accord with national policy, with local management guidelines as well as managers' and staff aspirations for the homes in which they work. Getting some agreement between these different players is critical.

AIM

The aim of the exercise is to help managers, field social workers, residential staff and elected members to identify their expectations for residential care. It should also shed light on barriers to effective practice.

Objectives are best agreed collectively. So important is the congruence between expectations about residence, it is worthwhile convening a half-day seminar bringing together representatives from each of the key players in a local authority. Ideally this should involve a manager responsible for determining the services children and families should receive, as well as a field social worker, residential staff and elected members. Where appropriate, children and family members could be included, although this would need very careful preparation and planning. A trainer or facilitator could be usefully employed to co-ordinate the work.

PRELIMINARY TASKS

Be familiar with summary 6.

THE EXERCISE

1 The discussion should centre on one home known to most of the group. Independent of each other, each person should complete the following sentence: 'The primary task of (the selected home) is to .....'
The written answers should be posted onto a flipchart. Discuss the different perspectives for 15 minutes.

2 As a group discuss what should happen in two specific situations. Who should take action and why:
• when a resident is about to go out without permission
• if one resident assaults another.
Spend 15 minutes on each situation. Break for 10 minutes.

3 Reconvene. Discuss whether there is agreement about what is best practice when a resident is about to leave the home without permission or when one resident assaults another.

4 In the light of these discussions ask:
• what are the similarities in the perspectives of different people in the local authority?
• what are the differences and why?
• can the differences be reconciled?
and finally,
• what impedes best practice?
• what helps best practice?

5 Consider whether the exercise suggests a need for action to achieve clearer definitions and more congruence in relation to local policy, procedures and guidelines.

5   How useful is the written statement of purpose and function?

Being clear about what residence can and cannot achieve on behalf of vulnerable children is at the heart of this publication. The written statements of purpose and function are the clearest exposition of these objectives.

AIM

The aim of the exercise is to help those responsible for residential services to look afresh at the written statements of purpose for selected homes.

It is best suited to those routinely required to read and comment upon the statement of purpose and function of a residential home, for example to service planners or operational managers. Typically, it might involve an area director together with the external and internal managers of selected homes. Elected members who know the home well could also make an important contribution. One person in the group should take a co-ordinating role.

PRELIMINARY TASKS

Be familiar with summaries 5, 6, 7 and 9.
The exercise is best undertaken on the basis of information collected from one or two residential centres. The exercise is not a test of the home. Choose one that is sufficiently confident to open itself up to external scrutiny.
The person co-ordinating the exercise should summarise in one paragraph the needs of each child at the point they came in to the home.
Photocopy the summary information on the children and the placement's statement of purpose and function for the True for Us group.

THE EXERCISE

1 The group should work through the following tasks:
• Read the summary information on the children
• Read the statement of purpose and function of the home
• Discuss whether it is likely that the placement, as it appears from the statement of purpose and function, is doing what is necessary to meet the needs of these children
• Where there are gaps, ask whether they reflect what the home actually does or what is written down in the statement.
This work should take about an hour. Break for 10 minutes.

2 The group should reconvene, this time to discuss the use of statements of purpose and function across the local authority. Ask:
• Does everyone connected with residential settings in the local authority know where to find the statement of placement and function? And are there opportunities for them to read and reflect upon it?
• If there are differences between children's needs and the statement of purpose and function, what should be changed, the children or the statement?
• If there are differences, what action needs to be taken by whom?

6 Bullying and sexual harassment between children

The research shows that most children bullied, sexually abused or harassed in residence are the victims of other children. Knowing this fact can improve the practice of individual staff. Knowing who is most likely to bully and who is most likely to be a victim can also enhance outcomes.

AIM

This exercise looks at the prevalence of bullying and sexual harassment between children and encourages reflection on strategies to reduce it.

It is for all staff within an individual residential setting. It can be co-ordinated by a front-line worker. Two children's homes might come together to compare results.

PRELIMINARY TASKS

Be familiar with pages 28-30 of the overview essay and with summaries 3, 7 and 10.

THE EXERCISE

The group should consider all the children in a home. (It may help to have a list of names.) Members of the group should answer these questions.

- Who talks about being bullied or harassed?
- What do they say?
- What is the context for the bullying/abuse?
- Where and when does it occur?
- What evidence is there?
- How are the victims recognised?
- What are the staff responsibilities in these situations?
- How do staff handle incidents
    at the time
    afterwards with those involved
    with the whole group of young people
    with family members
    with the staff group?
- What action should be taken on behalf of any vulnerable children (including those who bully and harass)?
- Consider what action could be taken to increase staff awareness and ability to deal with such situations.

7   The relationship of staff numbers and staff training to a home's purpose and function

A conclusion of this publication has been that too often the planning of residence has begun with the organisational requirements, followed by training and recruitment of staff with decisions about the placement of children coming after that. Much better to start with an understanding of the needs of the child, recruit staff accordingly, provide them with appropriate training and ensure that they are adequately supported by management.

AIM

The aim of this exercise is to help those responsible for residence to adopt this linear approach while not losing the strengths of existing services. It is best suited to a small group of line managers, external or internal. Very small authorities might collaborate with neighbours and compare results. The person in the authority responsible for the delivery of training should be involved and would be an ideal co-ordinator of the exercise.

PRELIMINARY TASKS

Be familiar with pages 27-32 of the overview essay and with summaries 5, 10 and 11 as well as the Regulation 4 and 5 (CHR 91) and associated guidance.

THE EXERCISE

1 Each line manager participating in the exercise should note for each of the homes for which they have responsibility (a) how many children are resident and, in a paragraph, enumerate their needs; (b) how many staff are employed and, in a paragraph, enumerate their skills, qualifications and training.

2 Using the information gathered from each home, the line manager should set out:
• what are needs for service and current care plans for each of the children resident in each home
• whether the mix of staff skills and qualifications suggests (i) over provision; (ii) under provision or (iii) a good mix as far as achieving the desired outcomes is concerned
• what changes to staffing and training does this exercise suggest?
• what capacity do staff have to be using their skills in different ways, for example, with outreach work?

3 The co-ordinator of the exercise should organise a meeting to enable the participating line managers to bring their results together (a) to see whether the strengths of some settings can offset the weaknesses of others (b) to discuss the possible implications for strategies towards residence in the authority as a whole.

8   Creating a staff culture that is in keeping with the objectives of residence

Many of the studies scrutinised the culture of children's homes. They considered whether homes might be said to have a positive culture, for example by asking if it provided a healthy living environment for the children and the staff.

AIM

The aim of this exercise is to encourage care staff to consider the importance of 'culture' as a route to increasing their understanding of how children's homes function. It can be undertaken by any small group comprising people with some experience of residential care. It is ideal for staff groups. A confident residential centre might invite in a field social worker or elected member to participate in the process.

PRELIMINARY TASKS

Read the definitions of culture in summaries 6 and 10.

THE EXERCISE

1 In the left hand margin of a sheet of paper write down the seven dimensions of the *Looking After Children* materials. Against each dimension, describe a predicament that ordinarily occurs inside a children's home or other residential centre. A list is given here as a guide.

Health *A resident complains of feeling too ill to get out of bed.*

Education *A resident asks for a quiet space in which to do homework.*

Social presentation *A 12-year old resident decides to have his/her nose pierced.*

Identity *A resident of mixed parentage asks about his/her ethnicity.*

Self care skills *A resident refuses to take regular baths or showers.*

Emotional and behavioural development *Two residents have a fight that results in one getting a black eye.*

2 Photocopy the sheet for each member of the group.

3 Each member of the group should write a paragraph about how they or their colleagues would respond to each of the seven events. This will take about 40 minutes. Take a 10 minute break.

4 When you come back together, assemble the results. Discuss areas of agreement and disagreement. If the exercise is being undertaken in a children's home, try to agree what it says for future practice and what action needs to be taken to support staff in their responses.

9   The relationship between external and internal management

As the role and size of the residential sector have changed over the last three decades, so its management ties with the larger organisation of the personal social services have come under strain. The Cardiff team have noted the potential isolation of many community homes.

AIM

This short exercise is designed to encourage managers of homes and other services to understand the connections between their work and to improve the level of collaboration between agencies. Since the aim is to reflect on the communication between different levels in the organisation it is helpful to have representatives of people from different layers and sectors. A mixture of managers, field social workers, residential staff, elected members will work. Representatives from health and education would be ideal.

PRELIMINARY TASKS

Read summary 12 and the section in the overview essay on management, inspection and training on pages 33-38.

THE EXERCISE

This exercise makes use of the results from Step 1 of Exercise 1. (Since it involves confidential information about children currently in residence, great care should be taken with any case material used.) The group should split into pairs. One person should take the role of the care manager or social worker co-ordinating case management from an area office; the second should take the role of a residential worker supporting the child.

1 Take one of the cases from Exercise 1 for whom services were specified in relation to needs, best and worst outcomes at Stage 3 of Exercise 1. Consider what the care manager and the residential social worker would do to ensure the service is delivered effectively.

2 Consider what tensions would be likely to exist between care managers, social workers and residential workers in the delivery of this service and how these tensions can be overcome.

3 Consider what management support would be needed to ensure that care managers and residential social workers can work effectively with each other, and ensure that services are delivered and outcomes properly monitored.

4 Repeat the sequence for the other cases. Each case should take about 15 minutes. Take a break after completing three.

5 Reconvene as a group. Chart the existing structure for managing residential care in the authority. Ask whether this is satisfactory for meeting the needs of the children being looked after. Suggest realistic changes to improve future outcomes. Consider how these may be taken forward.

This group exercise will take about an hour.

10 Management responsibilities for children absent from care or accommodation

The research shows that looked after children are more likely to run away than other children. Children who run away frequently commit offences and are also at risk of becoming victims of crime and sexual exploitation. Managers require mechanisms to know who is missing and to chart patterns of running away.

AIM

This exercise aims to encourage managers and heads of home to monitor the absences of looked after children from residential and foster care. It is for managers of out-of-home services provided by and on behalf of the local authority.

PRELIMINARY TASKS

Be familiar with page 41 of the overview essay and summaries 1, 3, 4 and 9. Whoever co-ordinates the activity will need to assemble as much information as there is available about six young people who have run away on at least one occasion.

THE EXERCISE

1 The following information ought to be collected for each absence. If a child has been absent several times, record the details on the same sheet of paper. If the information is not readily available record 'missing data'.
- the length of absence
- what (according to him/her) the child did when absent
- whom the absentee was with
- child's reason for absence(s)
- the number of previous similar absences
- the child's age at first unauthorised absence
- what action was taken immediately on return
- where (according to him/her) the child went when absent
- other information (eg from police or family on child's whereabouts and activities)
- who talked to him/her on return
- what strategy was adopted to resettle the child or move him or her elsewhere
- whether the child ran away again (if so, the questions should be answered afresh).

2 The group should spend an hour considering the information that has been assembled. Ask how the missing information can be uncovered for future cases. Consider any pattern that emerges and strategies for dealing with such incidents.

3 Effective management depends on knowing this amount about each child who runs away and ensuring it is routinely shared with other professionals and family members. Members of the group should individually find time to monitor patterns of running away at least every six months, eventually to provide:
- a risk assessment for each absent child and a plan to meet the particular needs of the child to minimise the frequency of absences
- a risk assessment for other children living with the absent child and a plan to support those caring for the child and others.

4 A week or so later, the group should reconvene and consider the findings of the work undertaken in 3. The end result should be to suggest ways of improving the management information system for runaway children as well as local policies and procedures.

11 Interprofessional working

Residential staff have to interact with a wide network of other professionals in order to meet the needs of children and young people. Sometimes the necessary work is done by field social workers or managers, sometimes by volunteers or relatives.

AIM

The aim of this exercise is to help staff who contribute to the care of children and young people to compare actual with 'ideal' practice planning, and to reconcile expectations with those of other professionals. The dimensions of a young person's development discussed are those used in the *Looking After Children* Assessment and Action Records. It is for mixed professional groups of 4-8 people. Involving elected members might give some leverage when it comes to recommendations for better practice. If the group is large, split into two for Stages 1 and 2, and reconvene for 3 and 4.

PRELIMINARY TASKS

Be familiar with summaries 9, 10 and 12.

THE EXERCISE

1 List by role all those professionals/workers who become involved in the health needs of children and young people in residential care.
Do likewise in relation to their:
- educational needs
- identity needs
- family relationship needs
- social presentation needs
- emotional and behavioural development needs
- self care needs.

Spend about 20 minutes on this stage.

A schematic representation of the 'working life space' of the staff of a children's home, from *Working in Children's Homes: Challenges and complexities* (Summary 10)

2 Draw a circle on a large sheet of paper, divide the area of the circle into segments and label the segments with all the roles identified at Stage 1. Again, about 20 minutes can be spent on this stage.

3 Display these 'life space' diagrams. Each group member in turn should select a young person in residential care whose case is known to them and, with their circumstances in mind, reconsider the diagrams. Add any additional roles to the diagram that may have been missed. Spend 10 minutes on this part of the work and then break for 10 minutes.

4 Reconvene for about an hour. In the light of what has emerged discuss:
- expectations of those who become involved in meeting the needs of children and young people
- what each of the group considers they can contribute
- how any mismatch between expectations might be improved.

Choose someone to bring together the life stage diagrams for the benefit of all the participants, and encourage general feedback about the lessons learned and the expectations of the professional groups.

12 Children in residence and their relations with their home environments

The research presented in this publication echoes that described in similar previous publications, namely that most children stay or hope to stay in touch with their home environment, most leave residence to live with relatives and most who try to live independently continue to draw support from family members. Practice concerning access and contact has been transformed since the 1989 legislation was implemented but there is still room for improvement. Moreover, since most separated children stay in touch with relatives, the situation of those who, for particular reasons, should not stay in touch becomes more salient. Contact, of course, can range from overnight stays, visits and meetings to telephone calls and letters.

AIM

This exercise is designed to focus professional attention on the issues surrounding questions of access, contact and identity. It can be completed by a group of three to five professionals which includes one or two with recent experience of supporting children looked after. The whole exercise will take about an hour.

PRELIMINARY TASKS

Be familiar with summaries 3 and 4. Where possible, glance at the Department of Health and Social Security's overview of child care research, *Social Work Decisions in Child Care*.

THE EXERCISE

1 A participant who has recently had responsibility for a looked after child should give a brief social history of the case.

2 The group should then ask the following questions:
- Who is the most significant supportive adult in the child's life?
- Who are the child's parents, grandparents, siblings and other significant relatives?
- What levels of contact (from none to living with) do they have with the child?
- What does each know about the child's needs and aspirations?
- What impact does this contact have on the child?
- Which contacts does the child value and why?
- If family members are excluded from the child, who else will provide the necessary supports?
- Who has asked the child whom he or she wishes to be in contact with?

3 Repeat with the process for other cases. Consider how current contact arrangements can be improved.

The young person's perspective

Many of the studies included in this overview have relied heavily upon children's perspectives of residential care. Sinclair and Gibbs sought the views of several hundred children living in 48 children's homes. Farmer and Pollock, Whitaker and colleagues among others spent time listening to residents' own accounts of life in the placements they studied. In *A Life Without Problems?* co-author Siobhan Kelly writes at length about her own experiences, before, during and after specialist intervention.

Encouraging children to be more involved in the development of services organised to meet their needs has been a recurring theme of this and previous programmes of research. Forward-looking authorities have employed children's rights officers to give structure to the involvement of children in need.

Dorothy Alexander, the children's rights officer in Durham, was a member of the advisory group and in this capacity showed summaries of the research studies to three young people and asked them to highlight 'key messages' for Social Services managers, policy makers, residential staff, social workers or trainers, and to other agencies such as Health and Education. The three either are or have been members of Care in Durham, a group run by young people who are or have been in care.

Their responses, extracts from which follow, give a clear indication that the research findings were 'true for them'. The level of their perception reinforces Sir William Utting's view in *People Like Us* that 'looking after them (young people) would be easier and much more effective if we really heard and understood what they have to tell us'. It is certainly unlikely that young people will stand in the way of any of the developments proposed in the conclusion and, as the final quotation suggests, their irritation may increase if constructive change does not occur.

'No-one should tolerate bullying–staff, young people or managers.'

'Every children's home should have a policy on bullying. As well, people in authority shouldn't bully by putting emergency placements in planned placement homes, because it makes everyone's life difficult. The staff don't know the young person's background. Young people feel intimidated. It's like living with a stranger in their home... Young people can be emotionally and physically abused... It makes things very very horrible and very very difficult.'

'Education is not just for five years; it affects your whole life.'

'When a young person goes into a children's home, in the planning the most important thing will be meeting the young person's educational needs. This means that the home, the social worker and the school teachers should have regular contact to keep up with any problems that occur, eg bullying, homework, lack of support. You need to stress the point that the young person has to help him/herself before anyone can help, because it's the young person's life you're dealing with–and that the residential worker, social worker and teacher will need to support the young person.'

'Have higher expectations of us.'

'Social services should have higher expectations of young people and of their success while in and out of care, for example, by believing they can get good exam results, go to college or university, get a good job (but remembering that young people in further education need support–emotional and financial). They need to build up our self esteem and confidence.'

'Listen to us, empower and value us.'

Give young people a say in the way a home is run and in the ethos behind it. This will give them a chance to feel empowered and valued and will reduce their feelings of isolation and rejection. Always thoroughly involve young people in the plans for their lives. Make sure their voice is always heard. Give them a stake in their lives

'Reduce the number of staff changes.'

'Looking at *Children's Homes Revisited* only four out of 136 staff still worked for the same employer. Come on, that's less than 4%! It makes it hard for young people to find, let alone to sustain some stability in their lives.

'Leaving care can be like a bereavement.'

'Young people should not leave a children's home until they feel ready to leave and they should be properly prepared and supported. Moving house is one of the biggest upheavals in anyone's life. When a young person leaves a children's home there should be a lot of contact between the young person and the staff, as it will often have been a valuable part of their life, and to lose that would be like a bereavement. Contact should not be on a rota, but at the young person's pace. The young person should visit the home when it is suitable and staff should visit the young person in their flat or house. This would encourage the young person to cope and be proud of what they've got.'

'Stop moaning, focus on the positives–move forward.'

'Stop moaning and going over time and time again what in essence has been known for years through repeated pieces of research and is common knowledge. Focus on the positives and address negatives using positive aspects as a platform. Use that vast information as a direction giver... A song that frequently comes into my head when looking at the slow rate of change in residential care is Del Amitri's *Nothing Ever Happens*. "The needle returns to the start of the song and we all sing along like before!"'

References

Bebbington, A. and Miles, J. (1989) 'The background of children who enter local authority care', *British Journal of Social Work*, XIX, pp.349-368

Berridge, D. (1985) *Children's Homes*, Oxford, Blackwell

Berridge, D. and Brodie, I. (1998) *Children's Homes Revisited*, London, Jessica Kingsley

Biehal, N., Clayden, J., Stein, M. and Wade, J. (1995) *Moving On: Young people and leaving care schemes*, London, HMSO

Brown, E., Bullock, R., Hobson, C. and Little, M. (1998) *Making Residential Care Work: Structure and culture in children's homes*, Aldershot, Ashgate

Bullock, R., Little, M. and Millham, S. (1998) *Secure Treatment Outcomes: The care careers of very difficult adolescents*, Aldershot, Ashgate

Bullock, R., Millham, S. and Little, M. (1993) *Residential Care for Children: A review of the research*, London, HMSO

Bullock, R., Gooch, D. and Little, M. (1998) *Children Going Home: The reunification of families*, Aldershot, Ashgate

Cliffe, D. and Berridge, D. (1992) *Closing Children's Homes: An end to residential child care?*, London, National Children's Bureau

Department of Health, *Children Accommodated in Secure Units*, Annual Publication

Department of Health, *Children's Homes at 31st March, England*, Annual Publication

Department of Health, *Children Looked After by Local Authorities, Year Ending 31st March*, Annual Publication

Department of Health (1989) *The Care of Children: Principles and practice in regulations and guidance*, London, HMSO

Department of Health (1991) *Patterns and Outcomes in Child Placement: Messages from current research and their implications*, London, HMSO

Department of Health (1991) *Residential Care for Children: Report of a Department of Health seminar*

Department of Health (1995) *Child Protection: Messages from Research*, London, HMSO

Department of Health (1997) *People Like Us: The report of the Review of Safeguards for Children Living Away from Home (The Utting Report)*, London, Stationery Office

Department of Health and Social Security (1985) *Social Work Decisions in Child Care: Recent research findings and their implications*, London, HMSO

Farmer, E. and Pollock, S. (1998) *Sexually Abused and Abusing Children in Substitute Care*, Chichester, Wiley

Gibbs, I. and Sinclair, I. (1998) 'Private and local authority children's homes: A comparison', *Journal of Adolescence*, XXI, 5

Hills, D. and Child, C. (1998) *Leadership in Residential Care: Evaluating qualification training*, Chichester, Wiley

Little, M. and Kelly, S. (1995) *A Life without Problems? The achievements of a therapeutic community*, Aldershot, Arena

Moss, P. (1975) 'Residential Care of Children: A general view' in Tizard, J., Sinclair, I. and Clarke, R., *Varieties of Residential Experience*, London, Routledge & Kegan Paul

Packman, J. and Hall, C. (1998) *From Care to Accommodation: Support, protection and control in child care*, London, Stationery Office

Parker, R., Ward, H., Jackson, S., Aldgate, J. and Wedge, P. (eds.) *Looking After Children: Assessing outcomes in child care*, London, HMSO

Rowe, J., Cain, H., Hundleby, M. and Keane, A. (1989) *Child Care Now: A survey of placement patterns*, London, British Agencies for Adoption and Fostering

Rutter, M., Maughan, B., Mortimore, P. and Ouston, J. (1979) *Fifteen Thousand Hours: Secondary schools and their effects on children*, London, Open Books

Sinclair, I. and Gibbs, I. (1998) *Children's Homes: A study in diversity*, Chichester, Wiley

Wade, J. and Biehal, N. with Clayden, J. and Stein, M. (1998) *Going Missing: Young people absent from care*, Chichester, Wiley

Ward, H. (ed.) *Looking After Children: Research into practice*, London, HMSO

Whipp, R., Kirkpatrick, I., Kitchener, M. and Owen, D. (1998) *The External Management of Children's Homes by Local Authorities*, Cardiff University Business School

Whitaker, D., Archer, L. and Hicks, L. (1998) *Working in Children's Homes: Challenges and complexities*, Chichester, Wiley

PUBLICATIONS OF THE DEPARTMENT OF HEALTH SUPPORT FORCE FOR CHILDREN'S RESIDENTIAL CARE

A Strategic Planning Framework: Part I - Analysing Need; Part II - Implementing change

Code of Practice for the Employment of Residential Child Care Workers

Contracting for Children's Residential Care: Part I -Overview; Part II- Guide to practice

Final report to the Secretary of State for Health

Good Care Matters: Ways of enhancing good practice in child care

Matching Needs and Services: The audit and planning of provision for children looked after by local authorities

Out of Authority Placements: Checklists of information to be obtained

Progress Report to the Secretary of State for Health - Planning and providing residential care for children

Recruitment and Staff Selection Techniques: Database

Specialising in Residential Child Care - A discussion paper

Staff Supervision in Children's Homes

The Use and Development of Databases of Residential Child Care Resources

Unit Costing and Financial Management in Children's Residential Care: Part I - Overview; Part II - Guide to practice also available from Wiley in the series

LIVING AWAY FROM HOME: STUDIES IN RESIDENTIAL CARE

Farmer, E. and Pollock, S. *Sexually Abused and Abusing Children in Substitute Care*

Hills, D. and Child, C. *Leadership in Residential Care: Evaluating qualification training*

Sinclair, I. and Gibbs, I. *Children's Homes: A study in diversity*

Wade, J. and Biehal, N. with Clayden, J. and Stein, M. *Going Missing: Young people absent from care*

Whitaker, D., Archer, L. and Hicks, L. *Working in Children's Homes: Challenges and complexities*

STUDIES IN THE DARTINGTON SOCIAL RESEARCH SERIES
available from Ashgate Publishing, Gower House, Croft Road, Aldershot, Hampshire GU11 3HR

Brown, E., Bullock, R., Hobson, C. and Little, M. *Making Residential Care Work: Structure and culture in children's homes*

Bullock, R., Little, M. and Millham, S. *Secure Treatment Outcomes: The care careers of very difficult adolescents*

OTHER PUBLISHED STUDIES INCLUDED IN THE PROGRAMME

Little, M. and Kelly, S. *A Life without Problems? The achievements of a therapeutic community* available from Arena, Gower House, Croft Road, Aldershot, Hampshire, GU11 3HR

Berridge, D. and Brodie, I. *Children's Homes Revisited* available from Jessica Kingsley Publishers, 116 Pentonville Road, London N1 9JB

Biehal, N., Clayden, J., Stein, M. and Wade, J. *Moving On: Young people and leaving care schemes*, available from The Publications Centre, PO Box 276, London SW8 5DT

Gibbs, I. and Sinclair, I. (1998) 'Private and local authority children's homes: A comparison', *Journal of Adolescence*, XXI, 5

Whipp, R., Kirkpatrick, I., Kitchener, M. and Owen, D. (1998) *The External Management of Children's Homes by Local Authorities*, Cardiff University Business School

Announcing an important new series, published by Wiley in association with the Department of Health...

LIVING AWAY FROM HOME
Studies in Residential Care

Photocopy this page to protect your book

Series Editors: Carolyn Davies, Department of Health, Lesley Archer and Leslie Hicks, University of York, and Mike Little, Dartington Social Research Unit, UK

- What happens to children who pass through residential care?
- How are homes run and what is it like to live and work in them?
- What is meant by quality in residential care and how does this affect outcomes for children?

Based on core studies in child care research commissioned by the Department of Health, the books in the series provide a balanced account of what life is like for children and staff in the majority of children's homes in the UK.

"Why not register your interest for the series and take advantage of 15% discount on your order!

To qualify, simply complete your details below and return to us to receive more information on books in the series plus confirmation of your 15% discount.

The other good news is that we offer a full Money Back Guarantee. So you can assess books in your own time, provided your books are returned within 30 days of receipt in a resaleable condition. So take the first step now and register for your 15% discount. We'll send you full details of books to choose from and make sure you're kept fully informed as the series grows."

Working in Children's Homes
Challenges and Complexities
DOROTHY WHITAKER, LESLEY ARCHER and LESLIE HICKS, University of York

On the basis of interviews and discussions with heads of homes and staff groups, the authors explore the tasks which face staff groups, the rationale for their procedures, their sources of stresses and rewards, and the everyday ups and downs characteristic of residential care.

0471 97953 8 262pp April 1998 Paperback £16.99

Leadership in Residential Child Care
Evaluating Qualification Training
DIONE HILLS and CAMILLA CHILD both of The Tavistock Institute, London, UK
Provides an account of the Residential Child Care Initiative - the only study to compare and assess the courses available for professional social work training. The authors illustrate and highlight the dilemmas concerning the provision of qualification training for residential care staff today, addressing issues such as the loss of qualified staff from the sector, and the debates concerning the model of "professional competence" that qualification training seeks to achieve.

0471 98477 9 200pp Spring 1999 Paperback £16.99

Sexually Abused and Abusing
Children in Substitute Care
ELAINE FARMER and SUE POLLOCK, School for Policy Studies, University of Bristol, UK
Provides a rich source of essential messages for policy and practice aimed at minimising the risks to these children and others. Drawing on information from a detailed study of 40 children, the authors explore the management of sexually abused and abusing children inside and outside their placements.

0471 98478 7 272pp September 1998 Paperback £16.99

Going Missing
Young People
Absent From Care
JIM WADE and NINA BIEHAL, with JASMINE CLAYDEN and MIKE STEIN, University of York, UK
Presents important findings from the first major study of young people who go missing from residential and foster homes. By exploring the diverse reasons why young people go missing and what happens when they do, the authors highlight the impact both of individual motivations and of residential and foster care contexts on the patterns associated with going missing.

0471 98476 0 232pp October 1998 Paperback £16.99

Children's Homes
A Study in Diversity
IAN SINCLAIR and IAN GIBBS, University of York, UK

This accessible text provides a much needed insight into the management of children's homes and the impact on their residents, drawing on perspectives from a large sample of children, parents, staff and social workers. It examines the effect on staff and residents of features such as size of home, staff ratios, proportion of trained staff and the approach of the head.

0471 98456 6 304pp September 1998 Paperback £16.99

Forthcoming in 1999...
Residential Care for Children:
Literature Review
IAN SINCLAIR

The External Management of
Children's Homes
RICHARD WHIPP and MARTIN KITCHENER

☐ **Yes, I wish to register for 15% discount on books in the Living Away from Home series:**

Title & Name _____

Job Title _____

Department _____

Company/University _____

Address _____

_____

_____

Post/zip code: _____ Country _____ e.mail _____

Daytime tel _____ Date _____

Now
FAX
(01243) 770638:
or post to
Tracy Clayton,
John Wiley & Sons Ltd,
Baffins Lane, Chichester,
West Sussex, PO19 1UD, UK.

Alternatively, to order, call our credit card hotline on (0800) 243407

Please quote reference 8008F when ordering